Client Assessment

edited by
Stephen Palmer and Gladeana McMahon

SAGE Publications
London • Thousand Oaks • New Delhi

Editorial selection © Stephen Palmer and Gladeana McMahon 1997
Introduction and Chapter 7 © Stephen Palmer 1997
Chapter 1 © Peter Ruddell 1997
Chapter 2 © Gladeana McMahon 1997
Chapter 3 © Berni Curwen 1997
Chapter 4 © Peter Ruddell and Berni Curwen 1997
Chapter 5 © Mark Aveline 1997
Chapter 6 © Patricia Armstrong 1997
Chapter 8 © Carole Sutton 1997

First published 1997

All rights reserved. No part of this publication may be
reproduced, stored in a retrieval system, transmitted or utilized
in any form or by any means, electronic, mechanical,
photocopying, recording or otherwise, without permission in
writing from the Publishers.

SAGE Publications Ltd
6 Bonhill Street
London EC2A 4PU

SAGE Publications Inc.
2455 Teller Road
Thousand Oaks, California 91320

SAGE Publications India Pvt Ltd
32, M-Block Market
Greater Kailash – I
New Delhi 110 048

British Library Cataloguing in Publication data

A catalogue record for this book is available
from the British Library.

ISBN 0 8039 7502 3
ISBN 0 8039 7503 1 (pbk)

Library of Congress catalog record available

Typeset by Mayhew Typesetting, Rhayader, Powys
Printed in Great Britain by Biddles Ltd, Guildford, Surrey

Contents

To the future generations: Kate, Tom, Emma, Leonora and Rebecca (SP)

To Mike, Thomas and Tigger (GM)

What Do You Say After You Say 'Er'?

Stephen Palmer

Just imagine for the moment that you are about to meet a new client. It may be easier if you recall the last time you did this.

What went through your mind? Perhaps you were thinking about your previous client; was it a good, a bad or an indifferent session? Maybe you were feeling thirsty as you had left yourself insufficient time to take a tea-break. Of course, it was not your fault that the previous counselling session went a few minutes over. The client just did not want to leave. In fact, perhaps you are feeling depressed and anxious like the client was? It's almost catching!

Are you thinking about the dinner party that you were organising that evening, or the wedding on Saturday? Could you find the new client's referral notes? Did you mislay them? In fact, could you remember the new client's name?

Hopefully this is *not* a familiar story, but seconds later you meet the new client and you show her into the counselling room. You inadvertently direct her to your chair with your assessment forms strewn all over your end of the room. You had placed the papers in front of the fan. 'You idiot! What's wrong with you today?' You can hear these words loudly inside your head. It's too hot to work. The air conditioning is not working. Neither is your brain. It's just not your day and this is a new client. What was her name?

> *Counsellor*: Er. It may be better if you sit here . . . My name is Stephen Palmer. [*At least you have remembered your own name. Yes, you are regaining your composure!*] Before we start, have you any questions you would like to ask me about myself or the Centre?

Jayne: No, not really. I received the details about the therapy you do and a sheet about yourself. I'm glad it's confidential. By the way, what is a psychotherapist? Is it the same as a shrink?

Counsellor: [*Oh no! This is the second time today I've been asked this question. This is a bad start.*] No. Unlike a psychiatrist I have not received training in medicine. In my case I help clients to deal with difficult problems that they are stressed about by using problem-solving strategies and also techniques to help reduce symptoms of stress. This referral letter from your occupational health department at work suggests that you are suffering from panic attacks. It may be a good idea if you give me an overview to the problems as you see them. [*Yes, you are beginning to focus on the job. The assessment starts.*]

Jayne: Well, it started about nine months ago. My boss gave me so much work to do. Even though I complained he paid no attention and after a couple of months I had to work long hours to reach the deadlines. But after six months of long hours I just could not go on. I felt so tired, yet I could not sleep properly. One day, I was in the lift at work and I thought I had a heart attack. I felt so awful, I almost fainted. Later the doctor told me that she thought it was a panic attack and then proceeded to give me beta blockers. They did not work. Now I get panics on the train as well as in confined areas at work. How can you help me?

Counsellor: . . .

Activity

Spend a few moments thinking about the following questions:

■ What would you say next?
■ Would you ask another question, summarise Jayne's reply in your own words, or stay silent?
■ Would you just nod your head or say, 'mmm'?
■ What would you be thinking?
■ What would you be feeling?
■ Would you share your thoughts and/or feelings with your client?
■ Would you give Jayne an assessment questionnaire to complete?
■ Would you share with Jayne how your approach to counselling would help her with her problem or would you keep this to yourself?

■ Would you wish you were somewhere else, with someone else, having an ice-cold drink? Would you share this thought with Jayne? Are you still thinking about the wedding or your previous client? (I hope not!)

The answer to these questions would probably depend upon your approach to counselling and perhaps on your personality too. (I would like to add that the scenario described does not necessarily reflect one of my counselling sessions.) Let us look at this subject further.

It's likely that the behaviour therapist may wish to undertake a behavioural analysis to see exactly what Jayne is avoiding. The cognitive therapist would be very interested in Jayne's cognitions (thoughts) and behaviours. The multimodal therapist would probably systematically examine different aspects of Jayne's personality in terms of seven modalities: behaviours, affects (emotions), sensations, images, cognitions, interpersonal relationships and drugs/biological factors. This is known by the acronym BASIC ID. The psychodynamic counsellor may be particularly interested in exploring earlier experiences and relationships as well as current conflicts. The person-centred counsellor may wish 'to "level" with the client, to show him that he is worthy of absolute attention, that he merits every effort the counsellor can make to understand him, that he is perceived as a fellow human being who, for that reason alone, can be assured of the counsellor's acceptance and honesty' (Mearns and Thorne, 1988: 100). Whatever the approach used by the counsellor, he or she is very likely to be working on building up a good therapeutic alliance with the client.

So How Can This Book Help?

The book is intended for both experienced and inexperienced counsellors, psychotherapists, psychologists and others working in the helping professions. Its intention is to give the reader an overview of the subject, taking a broad brush approach. In eight chapters the authors have covered a wide variety of issues relating to client assessment and later evaluation.

In Chapter 1, a range of general issues are covered including the nature of diagnosis, its benefits and the criticisms against it, and how your approach to counselling affects your assessment of your clients.

Chapter 2 is an introduction to client history taking and associated administration. Essentially, the chapter outlines what a counsellor needs to consider when embarking on client history taking and useful additional items such as client detail forms and information for clients about entering therapy. Chapter 3 focuses on medical and psychiatric assessment. This is one area of counselling and psychotherapy that is so often overlooked on counselling courses, yet may give counsellors a useful insight into psychiatric illness. This chapter covers the subject of suicide in some depth and how counsellors can assess clients for this particularly difficult problem.

The next two chapters focus on what interventions are available for clients. Chapter 4 concentrates on the type of help to give, whether the client being assessed is ready and suitable for counselling, and what may be the best setting for a client, for example individual or group therapy. This chapter looks at the practical issues, whilst Chapter 5, on assessing for optimal therapeutic intervention, covers three linked processes which need to be addressed: exploration, knowledge and planning.

The remaining three chapters show how to set goals, assess modalities, and review and evaluate therapeutic progress. Chapter 6, on assessment and accountability, looks at helping clients to set goals and at the assessment of whether the goals have been attained. Chapter 7 illustrates modality assessment and uses the BASIC ID framework (described earlier) developed by Arnold Lazarus. This comprehensive framework helps the counsellor and client to leave no stone (or modality) unturned. Exploration of each modality may help in establishing new therapeutic goals. It is particularly useful if counsellor and client have reached an impasse in therapy. Chapter 8, on reviewing and evaluating therapeutic progress, focuses on planning, implementing plans, review and evaluation and uses the mnemonic ASPIRE.

Some of the issues covered in the book are coming to prominence as many service purchasers are interested in time-limited therapy and cost-effectiveness. Whether we like it or not, our profession does not exist in a plastic bubble, isolated from the demands of society. We are expected to provide a professional service at all times and client assessment is one crucial area of counselling that is often neglected, especially on basic counselling courses. The aim of this book is to provide readers with new ideas and perspectives on client assessment.

Although the book has been written to a particular structure, the reader does not have to start at Chapter 1 and read through to Chapter 8. Each chapter can stand alone, and counsellors and therapists, experienced and inexperienced, may find a section of interest that they could use in their therapeutic work.

Reference

Mearns, D. and Thorne, B. (1988) *Person-Centred Counselling in Action*. London: Sage.

1 *General Assessment Issues*

Peter Ruddell

Dear Mr Ruddell

I am hoping you can point me in the right direction. My life feels a mess and there seems to be nothing but problems. My moods are up and down. My husband, Rajid, is always irritable with me. I think he may be having an affair, although he denies this and says he loves me. He constantly shouts at the children and I'm scared this may lead to the dreadful sort of upbringing which I've had. I feel I'm walking on eggshells. I think my husband needs help too.

I get so wound up but at least I can concentrate on my housework and can proudly say my house is spotless. This is my only sense of release at the moment.

Please can you help?

Yours sincerely

Jane Khan

What help might be offered to this person? Before deciding, it would be necessary to speak to her further. Even so, a number of hunches or hypotheses about the person and her problems will probably be held in suspension in the mind of an experienced counsellor. A sensitive assessment would precipitate the major problems actually requiring attention, so that both counsellor and client are clear about where help is and is not needed. In this and the chapters that follow, we hope to help you to develop ways of approaching this rather difficult process.

Assessment is part of the therapeutic process. Consequently, it is important that components of the counsellor/client relationship are not temporarily neglected during assessment. Hence, it will be helpful to apply to the assessment phase all those factors considered in your general practice, such as maintaining an appropriate degree of empathy and trust so as not to compromise the therapeutic relationship. Assessment literally means 'to sit by', and it may be helpful to remember this when faced with the prospect of eliciting information from a client.

Assessment may take place in a number of different ways. It will usually begin, even if only in a tentative form, at the first point of contact which may be at the telephone enquiry stage. I will discuss below how the particular therapeutic framework impacts on the mode and parameters of assessment.

First comes the preliminary assessment, or what the psychodynamic practitioner Malan (1979) terms the 'preliminary enquiry'. Malan suggests the aims of this phase are to discover

1 the exact nature of the fault
2 how it developed
3 other features which may shed light on what has gone wrong
4 what should be done to correct it.

He suggests that the assessment involves a system that is malfunctioning, in which an expert carries out a preliminary enquiry in order to identify what has gone wrong and then prescribes an appropriate intervention in order to try to set it right. Assessment is therefore concerned with the diagnosis of a problem, difficulty, disorder and so on.

Diagnosis involves matching signs and symptoms of your client with a known cluster of symptoms (a syndrome). Chapter 3, on psychiatric assessment, considers such a diagnosis in far greater detail. It is useful to familiarise yourself with the main groups of psychiatric disorder to ensure that the help given to your client is maximally effective.

The purpose of making a diagnosis is to allow the counsellor to intervene in the most effective way possible. Yet this is far more difficult than it first seems as people are complex and are part of wider systems such as family systems, social systems, economic systems, political systems and cultural systems. Change is only possible within the limitations set by the system or systems of which the person is a part and with the resources at the person's disposal. For this reason, a particular problem might have multiple remedies, or require intervention at many different levels. This is why it is so important to 'sit by' the client to discover why this person is here at this particular time, with this particular problem/ dilemma and with these particular resources and coping styles within this framework of functioning. (This concept of functioning within many different systems is considered for the intrapersonal level in Chapter 7.)

The Benefits of Diagnosis

Diagnosis is concerned with classifying a problem. Some counsellors are reluctant to classify problems in this way, and believe that individuals should not have signs and symptoms sectioned off and labelled. They believe this is to reify aspects of the person – to turn the person into a thing, an object of study rather than a complex changing individual.

Yet diagnosis is important if we are not to engage the individual in protracted 'therapy' for a problem which a given approach might never assist. For example, Malan – a psychodynamic therapist – has noted that 'there is no known authenticated case of an obsessional hand-washer being cured by psychoanalytic treatment' (1979: 107).

Diagnosis begins with a consideration of signs and symptoms. Signs are externally observable: sneezing, giggling, inability to make eye contact, loss of weight, protracted silences. Symptoms are subjective: headache, hearing voices not heard by others, or feeling 'low'. In medical diagnosis, it is common to detect the cause of the signs and symptoms (aetiology) as well as considering their development (pathogenesis). In psychiatric diagnosis, aetiology is more usually inferred. For example there is not a known cause of schizophrenia. While certain chemicals or hormones might be in evidence in the body of a person with heightened anxiety, these cannot be said to have caused the anxiety.

A psychiatric diagnosis therefore considers signs and symptoms of a client and matches them against a known category of disorder or dysfunction. For example, a person experiencing low mood, weight loss, insomnia, lack of energy and feelings of worthlessness might be diagnosed as suffering a major depressive episode. Severity and duration of symptoms and signs are particularly important. For example many people may have experienced most or all of the above symptoms at some time in their lives, but not all at once, or with insufficient severity or too fleetingly to enable the signs and symptoms to be termed a depressive episode.

Symptoms and signs grouped together in the above way as a cluster may be termed a syndrome, a disorder or a disease, and may represent differing levels of severity. But professional thinking over the definition of a disease, a disorder or a syndrome may change over time.

Classification manuals listing such signs and symptoms clusters are regularly updated. The two most commonly used manuals covering mental health problems are the *Diagnostic and Statistical Manual of Mental Disorders* (currently in its fourth edition, DSM IV), published by the American Psychiatric Association (1994), and the fifth section of the *International Classification of Diseases* (currently in its tenth edition, ICD 10), published by the World Health Organisation (1992).

Some people are relieved to receive a diagnosis, but many who have been 'given' a diagnostic label experience it as unhelpful or humiliating. Changed role and status, such as job loss and poverty, may contribute to a person feeling disempowered. Therefore, practitioners need to give much thought to the purpose of diagnosis and consider the usefulness of conveying a diagnosis to an individual in each and every case.

We have considered how psychiatric diagnosis requires a broad and deep knowledge of both signs and symptoms, as well as classification systems to match them against. Some professionals contend that only a practitioner – such as a psychiatrist – who has developed this level of detailed knowledge is likely to be sufficiently well informed to decide upon an accurate diagnosis. Few counsellor training courses devote much time to such study, and consequently many counsellors are ill equipped to make an informed diagnosis. In view of the problem of labelling discussed below, it is particularly important when a diagnosis is given that it is accurate and the person providing it is acting within his field of competence. This may be an important factor in ensuring that the most appropriate help is offered. Yet many professionals other than counsellors, such as those general practitioners (GPs) who have not taken psychiatry as one of the core components of their general practitioner training, may find it necessary to provide a diagnosis without consultation with a psychiatrist. There are many instances where a common problem, such as depression or anxiety, can be easily diagnosed, and where a person with advanced training in psychiatry need not be involved. The main difficulty here is that signs and symptoms may suggest a common problem to the inexpert eye instead of recognition of a rare (or less common) problem. Yet this can happen to psychiatrists inexpert in other fields. For example, I know of a case where the individual was simply treated for depression for several years: it subsequently transpired that she was suffering from a medical condition known as lupus which went untreated. (See Chapter 3, in which psychiatric problems resulting from other illnesses and as iatrogenic consequences of certain drug treatments are discussed.)

The public desire for greater knowledge about a range of issues has led to a welcome growth in self-help books in recent years. Many of these books have an element of self-assessment within them. For example, *The Feeling Good Handbook* (Burns, 1989: 49–60) has a short chapter entitled 'How To Diagnose Your Moods'. Other books are more exclusively focused on diagnosis, such as Bartlett (1987). The extent to which well written and well researched books on self-diagnosis are helpful or harmful depends partly on the person using them being able to absorb the information and match it against their own problems or symptoms. The efficacy of self-diagnosis is a complex issue worthy of future research.

Purposes of Diagnosis

There are three main purposes for making a diagnosis. The first is to identify what the problem is, so that appropriate intervention(s) can be made. Whereas diagnosis is concerned with finding commonalities between the symptoms and signs of the person before you, to compare with a classification, treatment is very much concerned with a biopsychosocial assessment (see later). This is an assessment of all sources of help available to this particular person at this particular time. Diagnosis is therefore concerned with similarities whereas treatment is very much concerned with individual differences.

The second reason for diagnosis is for research, with a view to improving interventions for future sufferers. Psychiatry is a very young science, and only in the last four decades has specific treatment for particular psychiatric problems been attempted. Unsurprisingly, psychopharmacology is primitive in comparison with general medicine, and is generally ameliorative rather than curative. Similarly it is only in more recent years that psychotherapy and counselling have begun to be subjected to scrutiny through various outcome studies (see Smith et al., 1980).

A third reason for diagnosis centres around knowledge, communication and memory. This includes communicating with other professionals as well as representing (and remembering) the outside world through specialised language. For example, a carpenter has a specialised language to represent the tools and materials with which he or she works. Some wood is called oak, other ash, maple or mahogany. These terms are probably known by people generally. Yet if a furniture-maker wishes to build a billiard table, he may specify 'Andaman padouk' for its colour and physical qualities. Similarly, a practitioner in the mental health field might use a label to indicate a particular type of problem, such as panic disorder without agoraphobia. Such terms can enable the practitioner to build up a body of knowledge around various diagnostic categories to guide their practice. In this way, it is hoped that the counsellor is less likely to employ interventions which have no chance of aiding the client, just as the furniture-maker will not use wood for a billiard table which will twist and warp!

It is important that this means of classification is not allowed to deteriorate into the process of reification noted above. The person seeking help may be suffering with signs and symptoms which can be given a certain name, such as schizophrenia, manic depression or post-traumatic stress disorder. The person, however, is not a schizophrenic or a manic depressive any more than a person suffering from influenza is a 'flu'! Associated with the process of reification is stigmatisation, which has been described by Goffman both in its general sense (Goffman, 1963) and as it applies to people in 'total institutions' (Goffman, 1974).

An allied criticism of psychiatric diagnosis comes from the anti-psychiatry school of thought. Thomas Szasz (1991) suggests that because most mental 'disorders' do not have a demonstrable physical pathology, they are not illnesses and hence should not, in his view, be the province of doctors. Szasz also makes the point that 'if mental illnesses are diseases of the central nervous system, they are diseases of the brain, not the mind' (1991: 1574). In noting that psychiatric diagnoses allude only to human behaviours, Szasz suggests that such diagnoses do not deprive the person of free will. However, a number of physical diseases do not have (known) gross pathology, while there are both genetic and biochemical grounds pointing, for example, to a physical basis for schizophrenia and depressive disorders.

The second main aspect of assessment, the biopsychosocial formulation, considers the unique characteristics of the individual with a view to aiding recovery or change. In this process the person is regarded holistically, in their entirety, which includes their individual strengths and weaknesses and their total resources such as family support, social networks, work and professional structures, interests and so forth. A clear guide to assessment written from a social work perspective, which recognises the importance of a holistic approach, can be found in Lukas (1993).

One attempt to explain the concept of the whole person – and indeed going beyond the individual – is the idea of systems. Much has been written about systems theory, and certain therapeutic models are largely based upon such a theory, for example, family therapy (see Minuchin et al., 1978).

From the perspective of assessment, the main point to grasp is that individuals function as wholes, although many different parts may be operating at any one time. A change to any part of the system is likely to have consequences, and lead to changes within other parts of the system. For example, an intervention focused upon a person's cognitive processes (thinking) is likely to be accompanied by an alteration in their affective (emotional) and behavioural systems – the process being interactive. This interaction of subsystems underlies the cognitive therapies. Chapter 7, on the assessment of specific modalities, also gives examples of the ways in which different subsystems operate together in particular ways.

While the person has a number of subsystems operating within her, she is also part of other systems: social, cultural, family and employment. The person is a subsystem too, and a change to the person (now the subsystem) is likely to bring about changes to those other, wider systems. Equally, changes in those wider systems are likely to affect the person. If this whole process can be kept in mind while assessing the person's potential for positive change, this will be very useful.

The biopsychosocial assessment is an attempt to view the individual from this wider perspective. This rather clumsy word is a collection of three other words: 'biological', 'psychological' and 'social'. Such an assessment acknowledges that a change in any part of the overall system will affect the person as a whole; for example a change in a person's cell formation, such as in cancer, is likely to lead to changes in their psychological systems too. While a particular subsystem (in this case biological) might initiate change in the individual, such change may nevertheless be mediated through other subsystems, such as psychological and social. For this reason, it is often futile to think of a particular problem as being biological *or* social *or* psychological. These different systems interact, and while a particular problem might be prompted by a particular subsystem (such as the biological), change may be effected through other subsystems or a combination of them.

Practice Points

Assessment is *part* of counselling: avoid temporarily neglecting good counselling practice during assessment.

The purpose of assessment is to identify problems and to identify possible solutions, which may be multiple.

Diagnosis matches the client's signs and symptoms against known clusters of signs and symptoms to discover if a match can be found. Severity and duration are important. The known clusters are given in classification manuals.

Be aware of the problems of labelling and stigmatisation.

The biopsychosocial formulation views the individual holistically and is particularly sensitive to the individual differences of each person. It recognises that individuals are part of multiple systems and therefore function at many different levels. Individuals also have many different parts operating within them. Interventions can therefore be focused at many different points.

The Manner of the Assessment: Theories of Mind

A challenge faced me in writing this chapter: assessment covers the total range of counselling approaches. It is important to appreciate that your particular model of counselling (that is the theoretical framework in which you trained) will make assumptions about the nature of the human condition – about what it means to be human. These assumptions will fundamentally colour the counsellor's beliefs about the nature of the problems for which people seek help, the type of intervention which should be offered and the significance and meaning of the relationship between you and the person you hope to assist.

The range of different psychological therapies is extensive and continues to proliferate (Karasu, 1986). It is important to understand where your particular therapy fits into the overall pattern of therapies: what are the fundamental beliefs it is based upon, and what distinguishes it from similar therapies? It can also be useful to understand the major points of concurrence and disagreement with other therapies. The acquisition of this type of knowledge is important because it will help you to develop a broad framework within which to understand counselling more fully and to help you recognise where different approaches may be largely incompatible. A full discussion of these issues is beyond the scope of this book, but we will consider some aspects of three major therapeutic systems to understand how they might affect the process of assessment.

In the psychoanalytic framework (after Freud, 1916) the client (analysand) expresses their fears and wishes to the analyst through free association: 'he should report his thoughts without reservation and . . . he should make no attempt to concentrate while doing so' (Rycroft, 1968: 54). In a transference relationship with the therapist, the client displaces feelings, attitudes and impulses of earlier relationships onto the therapist. This is aided by the therapist being relatively neutral and anonymous. Through interpretations of this transference by the analyst, the client comes to recognise earlier conflicts and thus adopts a more appropriate (that is, non-transferential) relationship with others. Symptoms are usually seen as expressions of such intrapsychic conflict, that is conflict between two parts of the same mind, in contrast to conflict between two persons (1968: 77). A clear guide to psychodynamic counselling which does not assume an implicit knowledge of the field can be found in Jacobs (1988).

The person-centred framework (after Rogers, 1951) finds the therapist relating to the individual before her as unique and worthwhile (unconditional positive regard). She is empathic: she tracks the reality and experience of the individual from moment to moment to enable the client to do so as well. She is also congruent: she is accurately aware of her own feelings and shares them as appropriate. It is through this real relationship that change is seen to take place.

The cognitive-behavioural framework is psychoeducational (Ellis, 1984). The therapist brings his technical skill and experience to the client's problems. The client and therapist decide together which problem(s) require therapeutic attention. The therapist explains the cognitive-behavioural framework to the client who is gradually helped to test out unhelpful patterns of thought and behaviour. The relationship, though important, is not viewed as the sole means of change; rather, it is a vehicle for change.

These three contrasting approaches all have implications for assessment. For example, the cognitive-behavioural therapist might help the client to change patterns of behaviour or thinking in order to overcome symptoms such as panic attack (agreed as the goal of therapy by client and therapist). The psychodynamic practitioner may see the symptoms as secondary and the removal of them through cognitive-behavioural therapy as suppressing the real cause – intrapsychic conflict. Here the symptoms are seen as a defence against such conflict becoming conscious and over- whelming. A psychodynamic assessor might weigh ego strength against defences, and so on. From this perspective, the client would be best helped by recognising the nature of the hidden feelings as well as the feared consequences of expressing them. These insights are gained through the therapist's interpretations.

The person-centred therapist would view the problem as one of incongruence or inauthenticity: the client would come to recog- nise his fears and feelings through the medium of the relationship with the counsellor. The concepts of assessment, diagnosis and treatment are seen by most person-centred therapists as com- promising 'genuineness' – a cornerstone of the person-centred framework – as the client is viewed in an objective manner. A major person-centred objection is to expertise: it is anathema to think that an 'expert' knows another person better than she knows herself. To such a therapist, 'treatment' may imply that a counsellor 'does' something to the client and may consequently regard it as an implicit abuse of the client's humanity. A fuller consideration of the therapist's orientation will be found in Chapter 5.

Therefore, both the psychodynamic and person-centred frameworks are to some extent unitary, concentrating on past conflicts and current relationships respectively, whereas cognitive-behavioural therapies focus on thoughts and behaviour associated with the panic attack, derived from a detailed assessment. Nevertheless, a broad view should be taken at the assessment stage so that various resources and solutions may be considered.

So far, I have spoken of assessment as if it were a unitary phenomenon, underpinned by the counsellor's therapeutic approach. But there are a number of different ways in which assessment might take place.

General Assessment

A general assessment is usually undertaken in the first counselling session by a counsellor or in a clinic by a member of a mental health team. Where it is the person's first contact for the problem, it may be preferable for a full or at least partial history and assessment to be carried out as outlined in Chapters 2 and 3. Some counsellors object to assessment on the grounds that it is harmful to the relationship or to the person (see Rowan, 1983: 11–20), or on the grounds that it is inefficient (Dryden, 1991). Nevertheless, there will often be an implicit assessment about whether the person will remain in therapy and will be able to benefit from it, as Rowan (1983: 25–30) himself points out. Often, the counsellor will have received a referral from some other source, such as a GP. It is helpful to be aware of the salient aspects of previous relevant documentation prior to your first session. (The client's first contact is often with a GP, who only allocates an average of seven minutes for each individual seen. If he has referred the person on for specialist help, such as to a consultant psychiatrist, it is not uncommon for the two sources of information to identify different core problems!)

If you work for an agency which practises in a particular problem area, such as bereavement, AIDS or alcohol abuse, or which practises in a particular therapeutic framework such as cognitive-analytic, multimodal or rational emotive behaviour therapy, it is best for your agency's literature to give as much information as possible about the approach, to allow the user to make an informed choice. Some agencies may not use formal assessment for the reasons given above, or for reasons specific to the particular agency. For example, student counsellors may not do so because students may find the process alienating. The general assessment, when carried out, usually takes place in the first session, but in more complex cases might well go beyond this.

It is reasonable to meet the person in the reception area and show them to the counselling room. It is best if the room is reasonably airy, warm and uncluttered, with comfortable chairs. A box of tissues is usually considered essential! Take all reasonable precautions to ensure that you are not distracted once the session commences: disconnect telephones, ensure nobody will knock at your door and make certain you are not required to answer intercom systems. The room will hopefully be well insulated acoustically to prevent sound entering or leaving, particularly if it adjoins a reception area. With growing concerns over physical violence, books considering the issues surrounding violence and offering practical guidance have emerged (Breakwell, 1989). Safety is important and some counselling centres have taken measures to protect staff by the adoption of appropriate procedures and equipment (see Chapter 3).

It is important to inform the potential client that the first session will differ from the others as it *is* an assessment and may be almost entirely focused on collecting information about the client, their reason(s) for coming to you and their resources. Nevertheless, a reasonable balance should be struck between gathering information (task orientation) and attending to the client's feelings (person orientation) (Zaro et al., 1977).

Different practices are adopted in the initial assessment of a potential client. Some organisations operate an intake system where one counsellor does all the initial assessments. This has the advantage of matching particular counsellor skills with client problems and is a practice which many specialist agencies adopt (see Chapter 4). It is helpful to let the potential client know the following during the first session, as well as the reasons, where appropriate:

- whether or not you will be able to offer her counselling
- whether or not your organisation will be able to offer her counselling
- whether or not you or your organisation will be able to refer her to another agency for help.

It may not always be possible for you to give this information in the first session. For example, if you are relatively inexperienced, you may first need to discuss it with your supervisor. In such cases, this can be shared with the client.

The session usually lasts for an hour. (The conventional thera-peutic hour is 50 minutes, which allows 10 minutes to make notes.) A vast amount of information can be conveyed in this time and it needs to be recorded accurately. This can be achieved by writing notes immediately after the session, perhaps making brief notes during the session. All of your senses should be focused on the client, and this includes your eyes which will observe body language. Therefore it is important not to direct your gaze at a note-pad. Some counsellors audio-record the session and give the client the opportunity to do so too. This is beneficial as the recording can be used for supervision: a supervisor can gain a different view of a session from a tape than from a counsellor's recollection! I have seldom found the taping of sessions to be problematic, but would be flexible if a client did not favour such a practice. I always explain the reason for the tape – in order to aid supervision and to increase the effectiveness of therapy – before starting. Problems encountered in tape-recording a session often lie with the counsellor! Perhaps the most common difficulties relating to this problem are as follows: first, failing to provide an adequate rationale to the client; and second, the therapist's own lack of clarity or confidence about such use of tape-recording. As with all records, the tape should be carefully and confidentially stored. It is preferable to identify the person on the tape not by name or initials, but by code. In the event of theft or loss of the tape, this would further minimise the likelihood of unfortunate consequences for the client.

Confidentiality is an important issue. The British Association for Counselling suggests the following in its *Code of Ethics and Practice for Counsellors*: 'Counsellors should take all reasonable steps to communicate clearly the extent of the confidentiality they are offering to clients. This should normally be made clear in the pre-counselling information or initial contracting' (1993: B.4.6). If your client expresses an intent to perform an illegal action, you may be faced with a dilemma, especially where harm to another person is intended. In such cases, you are advised to carefully consider the code of ethics of your professional body. In some cases you may be bound by law to take appropriate action, for example where terrorism is involved. Where there are grounds for believing that the client will cause serious bodily harm, the BAC *Code* suggests that 'the client's consent to a change in the agreement about confidentiality should be sought whenever possible unless there are also good grounds for believing the client is no longer able to take responsibility for his/her own actions. Whenever possible, the decision to break confidentiality agreed between a counsellor and client should be made only after consultation with a counselling supervisor or an experienced counsellor' (1993: B.4.4). Similarly, intent to self-harm should be explored where appropriate and necessary action taken (see Chapter 3).

Once the problems have been assessed, it is necessary to assess the resources available to deal with them. These two aspects are very closely interwoven and it is very important to keep both in mind as the session proceeds. Chapter 4 discusses this in detail.

The Pros and Cons of Assessment

I noted above some of the wider objections to assessment, such as the problems of diagnosis and stigmatisation and the related problem of 'assessment' putting the therapist into the role of 'expert' rather than being 'genuine'. In the latter case, the person-centred counsellor might dispense with the 'assessment' (particularly as in Chapters 2 and 3), and embark instead on a collaborative negotiation with the client in a non-directive fashion. This is part of an argument which holds that 'assessment' leads the counsellor to act outside of their client's frame of reference: by being outside of the relationship with the client, the relationship is jeopardised. As the relationship is seen not only as the vehicle but as the main means through which change is accomplished, therapy too is jeopardised. This view (Hobson, 1985: 174) holds that the assessment process may replicate the lack of respect and empathy which the client has previously experienced and is a determining factor in the client's current problem. Similarly, if the externality which assessment implies is evident to the client, he or she may not trust the counsellor sufficiently to disclose important material.

In discussing the benefits of diagnosis earlier, I considered the idea that a particular problem could be isolated (diagnosis) and treatment based on the most probable outcome for that problem (prognosis) be given. Yet some practitioners (Szasz, 1991) fundamentally disagree with such a view, suggesting that at best a sufficiently comprehensive system of classification has not yet been achieved. Others believe it is impossible to arrive at. Certain adherents of this most extreme view see emotional disturbance as ensuing from a unitary process, requiring a single method of treatment across all problems. (Psychoanalysis is such a unitary approach.) For Patterson (1974) the human interpersonal relationship is the medium. Disputing the view of specific treatments for specific problems from an altogether different perspective, Liberman suggests that individual differences are too great to allow such solutions, which he believes are 'fatuous and unlikely to come to pass' (1981: 231).

The clinical assessment is carried out in order that a certain range of information is elicited, including crucial factors both contributing to the problem and contributing to possible solutions. Yet Dryden takes 'the view that although assessment interviews . . . may at times be useful in exploring clients' disturbances, perhaps the best form of assessment consists of having several [rational emotive behaviour therapy] sessions with the client' (1991: 52). But I have known some experienced therapists who have failed to recognise a significant problem – in one case alcohol dependency – as a result of not completing a comprehensive assessment at the outset.

There are other reasons for not completing a full assessment as previously outlined. For example it may be inadvisable owing to the client's current mental condition. This may be either on the grounds that information elicited will not be accurate, as for example with a person in deep psychosis, or on the grounds that the assessment may itself be damaging to the client in their current mental condition, such as a person who has just experienced severe trauma. In these cases, minimal assessment may be carried out or assessment postponed to a more appropriate time: it is advisable to make detailed notes of the observed features, or circumstances, leading to this decision, as discussed in Chapter 3.

I have so far implied that assessment is a one-off full assessment. However, there will be times when assessment will be directed not at the person's overall problem, but at a particular aspect of it. For example a full behavioural assessment might be necessary for a person suffering obsessive compulsive disorder (OCD) who repeatedly cleans certain areas of her house or body. In some cases, such detailed assessment might itself take several sessions by a trained behaviour therapist. As noted elsewhere in this chapter, the therapeutic framework influences the form of assessment undertaken.

Other circumstances in which minimal assessment might be appropriate are where the assessment is not for the immediate purpose of working with the client therapeutically, but is for determining the client's suitability for a particular agency, such as a day centre. Here, for example, assessment may be abridged, and may involve the client's participation with other users of the service.

While a general and comprehensive assessment of a client's problem will usually be made at the outset, an ongoing process of assessing the client's progress over the course of therapy will also be necessary. Depending on the type of therapy being offered, such ongoing assessment might be based upon reviewing the client's goals and problems (see Chapter 8).

Practice Points

Counselling can be thought of as a system, the different 'schools' or frameworks of counselling as subsystems. Remember assessment, too, is a subsystem overlaying these various approaches, and being altered by each of those it interacts with.

General assessment usually happens in the first session. It is helpful to have general information about your approach available in the form of leaflets which can be sent in advance.

Take care to attend to the physical environment in which the assessment will take place.

Discuss the reasons for the assessment and the components within it with your client.

Be clear what information you will (and will not) give to your client at the end of the assessment session(s), about future counselling sessions, and so on.

Keep an accurate record of the assessment session.

Confidentiality between client and counsellor: be guided by the code of ethics of your professional organisation. Whenever possible, the decision to break confidentiality should be made only after consultation with your counselling supervisor.

Transcultural Issues

I started this chapter by emphasising that assessment is embedded within the overall process of counselling, and demonstrated that the counselling process is itself embedded within the counsellor's theoretical framework or model. Three prominent approaches were outlined: cognitive-behavioural, psychodynamic and person-centred. Systems theory was also discussed. If you imagine these three approaches as subsystems of counselling, then assessment can be thought of as a larger subsystem overlaying them (Figure 1.1). I leave you to ponder where a 'bubble' for culture would be best placed. It probably does not cover all of counselling, yet is larger than counselling itself. It needs to overlay the different frameworks and also overlay assessment.

As an exercise, ask yourself how large, what shape and in what position the 'bubble' representing culture should be. Please

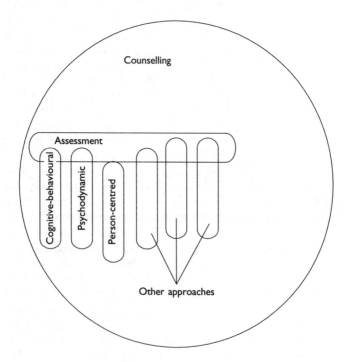

Figure 1.1 *Counselling system*

consider this before reading on, and keep your response in mind as you do so.

There are difficulties in trying to identify common therapeutic factors across widely different models of counselling, but the following have been proposed as essential elements for the counsellor (Truax and Carkhuff, 1967):

1 Be accurately empathic.
2 Be 'with' the client.
3 Be understanding, or grasp the client's meaning.
4 Communicate empathic understanding.
5 Communicate unconditional positive regard.

It is difficult to imagine that a counsellor could demonstrate any of these aspects if he or she is unable to communicate effectively with the client. If the cultures of the counsellor and the client are quite different, good communication will not be possible unless the counsellor makes a determined effort to understand the client and learn from the client. For even if the counsellor understands the client's words, their real meaning may evade the counsellor. This is because the client is part of a cultural system and meaning is culturally and socially constructed. The counsellor's own cultural and social systems may be xenophobic, and this is best acknowledged. Assessment across cultures can therefore be problematic. Rack (1982), for example, has noted in considerable detail some of the problems involved in the mere recognition of disorders such as anxiety, depression, mania, schizophrenia, paranoia and hysteria in people who are not from white American or European cultures by someone who is. Signs and symptoms often have culture-specific meanings. The use of standardised psychometric instruments across cultures has been shown to be highly questionable (MacCarthy, 1988) and has contributed to some practitioners rejecting such assessment approaches (Parker et al., 1995).

There is insufficient space in this introductory chapter to fully outline transcultural assessment. It is important to recognise it within the more general context of transcultural counselling, which emphasises 'the common experiences and tasks facing clients and counsellors, who are aware that their assumptions and practices are not absolute' (d'Ardenne and Mahtani, 1989). The work just cited is a good introduction to transcultural counselling.

In practice, it is important for the counsellor engaged in trans-cultural assessment to be particularly flexible and to discuss with the client the reason for the assessment and for the components within it. By acknowledging the client's right to be understood fully, and recognising that the probable power imbalance between counsellor and client is likely to be magnified across cultures, the effective counsellor will reach out to find a common framework for both cultures (Lonner and Sondberg, 1995). She will accept that language difficulties between counsellor and client are an important hindrance to effective communication and that other differences such as body language and diverse meaning systems across cultures present further challenges. The adequate counsellor will be proactive but sensitive in seeking an awareness of cultural variations, and in respecting the client she will be willing to accept that she has social and cultural biases of her own. By working sensitively in this way, the counsellor will deepen and enrich her practice.

Practice Points

Assessment, diagnosis and the use of psychometric instruments across cultures present special problems.

Accept that you have cultural and social biases of your own.

Recognise that power imbalances between client and counsellor are magnified across cultures.

Be proactive but sensitive in seeking an awareness of your client's culture: acknowledge your client's right to be understood.

Recognise that your assumptions and practices are not absolute and reach out to find a working framework of meaning common to the cultures of your client and yourself.

Measures used in Assessment

When assessing a person and their problems, it is not unusual – particularly in the cognitive-behavioural domain – to wish to measure the person's problem or some aspect of it. For example, if the client lacks assertiveness skills, it may be helpful to identify in what particular situations, and to what extent, she needs to improve those skills. Important reasons for measuring such aspects are that the individual can better appreciate the extent of the problem (and recognise that it has limitations), change can be monitored more thoroughly, time need not be wasted on areas where the client does not require, or wish for, change, and progress can be monitored and given tangibility (which is often particularly helpful in reminding the client of the progress made when setbacks occur).

A number of different methods exist to measure client problems: behavioural observations, in which a particular behaviour is measured in terms of its frequency, duration or interval; self-anchored scales such as SUDS (subjective units of distress: Wolpe and Lazarus, 1966) where the client assesses a quality by using a scale, such as rating their anger or distress in different situations on a scale from 1 to 9; rating scales, which are the same except that another person carries out the rating; client logs, which are essentially mini-journals detailing particular aspects of a problem; various unobtrusive measures such as a one-way mirror as commonly used in family therapy; electromechanical measures such as bio-feedback machines to aid relaxation training; and standardised measures, which consist of a series of structured questions or statements designed to elicit information from a person, such as the General Health Questionnaire (Goldberg, 1972).

Some practitioners, such as Bayne (1993), commend the use of the Myers-Briggs Type Indicator (MBTI) both for assessment purposes and also for exploring 'the possibilities of quicker and deeper empathy, more appropriate challenging, a wider range of strategies, and which kinds of strategies are most and least likely to be effective with which clients' (1995: 95).

A number of the standardised measures come with very detailed manuals, and it is neither advisable nor ethical to use them without the specialised training required.

In recent years, assessment measures have become more widely used and accepted, and this is partly due to the development of a wide range of standardised measures, known as rapid assessment instruments (RAIs) (Levitt and Reid, 1981). These are usually completed by the client, are short, simple to use and understand, rapidly scored and easily interpreted, and do not require the counsellor to have extensive knowledge of testing procedures. They provide an overall score giving an index of the magnitude of the problem, but are also useful in providing information from the individual items which can be used as material in therapy. They may be used with a client once only, or can be used repeatedly, enabling change over time to be focused upon. The range of RAIs is vast, and the counsellor would be advised to ensure that an instrument is chosen which is adequately validated (it assesses what it is designed to assess) and reliable (the items consistently measure the same entity). A detailed consideration of RAIs, together with a comprehensive sample of instruments, is given by Corcoran and Fischer (1987).

Practice Points

Numerous methods exist to measure clients' problems, or aspects of them.

Measurement helps

- clients to recognise the extent of a problem and that the problem has limits
- client and counsellor to monitor change
- time to be given to areas requiring change and not wasted on other areas
- progress to be monitored and given tangibility (which is helpful in setbacks).

Rapid assessment instruments (RAIs) are usually completed by the client and do not require the same rigour as standardised assessment measures. They can be used flexibly in a variety of ways.

Ensure any instruments you use are adequately validated and reliable.

Conclusion

This chapter has briefly considered a number of the broader aspects of assessment, emphasising that it is embedded within the overall context of counselling. I have also stressed that counselling practice is itself underpinned by the philosophical assumptions – the particular 'theories of mind' – to which each different type of counselling subscribes. Other subjects considered within this chapter have been diagnosis and the use of classification manuals, systems theory, the problem of labelling, transcultural issues, as well as measures used in assessment. Some practical guidelines have also been suggested. The following chapters will now consider some of these and other aspects in greater detail. Many of the subjects discussed in these pages will be suitable for lifetime study.

References

American Psychiatric Association (1994) *Diagnostic and Statistical Manual of Mental Disorders* (4th edn). Washington, DC: APA.

Bartlett, S.J. (1987) *When You Don't Know Where to Turn: a Self Diagnosing Guide to Counseling and Psychotherapy.* Chicago: Contemporary Books.

Bayne, R. (1993) 'Psychological type, conversations and counselling', in R. Bayne and P. Nicholson (eds), *Counselling and Psychology for Health Professionals.* London: Chapman and Hall.

Bayne, R. (1995) 'Psychological type and counselling', *British Journal of Guidance and Counselling,* 23(1): 95–105.

Breakwell, G.M. (1989) *Facing Physical Violence.* London: BPS Books and Routledge.

British Association for Counselling (1993) *Code of Ethics and Practice for Counsellors.* Rugby: BAC.

Burns, D.D. (1989) *The Feeling Good Handbook.* Harmondsworth: Penguin.

Corcoran, K. and Fischer, J. (1987) *Measures in Clinical Practice.* New York, London: Free Press.

d'Ardenne, P. and Mahtani, A. (1989) *Transcultural Counselling in Action.* London: Sage.

Dryden, W. (1991) *Reason and Therapeutic Change.* London: Whurr.

Ellis, A. (1984) 'Rational emotive therapy', in R.J. Corsini (ed.), *Current Psychotherapies.* Ilasca, IL: Peacock.

Freud, S. (1916) *Introductory Lectures on Psychoanalysis* (standard edn). London: Hogarth, 1963.

Goffman, E. (1963) *Stigma: Notes on the Management of Spoiled Identity.* Harmondsworth: Penguin.

Goffman, E. (1974) *Asylums.* Harmondsworth: Penguin.

Goldberg, D. (1972) *Manual of the General Health Questionnaire.* Windsor: NFER.

Hobson, R.F. (1985) *Forms of Feeling.* London: Tavistock.

Jacobs, M. (1988) *Psychodynamic Counselling in Action.* London: Sage.

Karasu, T.B. (1986) 'The specificity versus non-specificity dilemma: toward identifying therapeutic change agents', *The American Journal of Psychiatry,* 143: 687–95.

Levitt, J.L. and Reid, W.J. (1981) 'Rapid-assessment instruments for practice', *Social Work Research and Abstracts,* 17: 13–19.

Liberman, R.P. (1981) 'A model for individualising treatment', in L.P. Rehm (ed.), *Behaviour Therapy for Depression.* New York: Academic Press. p. 231.

Lonner, W.J. and Sondberg, N.D. (1995) 'Assessment in cross-cultural counseling and therapy', in P. Pederson (ed.), *Handbook of Cross-Cultural Counseling and Therapy.* Westport, CT: Greenwood Press.

Lukas, S. (1993) *Where to Start and What to Ask: an Assessment Handbook.* London: Norton.

MacCarthy, B. (1988) 'Clinical work with ethnic minorities', in F. Watts (ed.), *New Developments in Clinical Psychology,* vol. 2. British Psychological Society. Chichester: Wiley.

Malan, D.H. (1979) *Individual Psychotherapy and the Science of Psychodynamics*. London: Butterworths.

Minuchin, S., Rosman, B. and Baker, L. (1978) *Psychosomatic Families*. Cambridge, MA: Harvard University Press.

Parker, I., Georgaca, E., Harper, D., McLaughlin, T. and Stowell-Smith, M. (1995) *Deconstructing Psychopathology*. London: Sage.

Patterson, C.H. (1974) *Relationship Counselling and Psychotherapy*. New York: Harper and Row.

Rack, P. (1982) *Race, Culture, and Mental Disorder*. London: Routledge.

Rogers, C. (1951) *Client-Centred Therapy*. London: Constable.

Rowan, J. (1983) *The Reality Game*. London: Kegan Paul.

Rycroft, C. (1968) *A Critical Dictionary of Psychoanalysis*. Harmondsworth: Penguin.

Smith, M.L., Glass, G.V. and Miller, T.I. (1980) *The Benefits of Psychotherapy*. Baltimore: Johns Hopkins University Press.

Szasz, T. (1991) 'Diagnoses are not diseases', *The Lancet*, 338: 1574–6.

Truax, C.B. and Carkhuff, R.R. (1967) *Towards Effective Counseling and Psychotherapy: Training and Practice*. Chicago: Aldine.

Wolpe, J. and Lazarus, A.A. (1966) *Behaviour Therapy Techniques*. New York: Pergamon.

World Health Organisation (1992) *International Classification of Diseases* (10th edn). Geneva: WHO.

Zaro, J.S., Barach, R., Nedelman, D.J. and Dreiblatt, I.S. (1977) *A Guide for Beginning Psychotherapists*. Cambridge: Cambridge University Press. p. 41.

2 *Client History Taking and Associated Administration*

Gladeana McMahon

Basic Principles

Client history taking can be approached from a number of different angles depending on the orientation of the counsellor, the time constraints surrounding the counselling offered and the problem area presented by the client. A psychodynamically trained counsellor will tend to focus on early family history whereas a cognitive-behavioural counsellor will generally require detailed information about the current thinking and behaviour associated with the presenting problem. A counsellor may be constrained by agency policy and/or the number of available sessions, and these constraints will influence the emphasis of the type of history taken. If the client is seeking careers counselling, the history the counsellor takes will be affected by the type of problem presented.

When considering client history taking, there are four questions to be asked and answered:

1 What information do I require to help me assess the therapeutic needs of my client?
2 Is it better to elicit the information verbally, in written form, or through a mixture of the two?

3   Am I the best person to be working with this client or would it be more useful to refer them elsewhere (see Chapters 4 and 5)?
4   Does this case require me to liaise with any other agency and if so in what way?

This last question attempts to take into account inter-agency liaison, which is quite common in psychiatric, social and proba- tion work. The counsellor or counselling agency needs to have a clear policy regarding appropriate procedures such as confidenti- ality, responsibilities, individual and agency boundaries and any codes of ethics adhered to.

Referral Letters

Referral letters are common and come in many forms. Some con- tain detailed information whilst others provide (after giving name, address and date of birth) a brief single line statement, such as 'I would be grateful if you could see this patient who is anxious and depressed.' Some counsellors do not read referral letters until after they have seen the client for an assessment session as they do not want to be unduly influenced by what they read. Referral letters can sometimes be misleading as the impression the referrer has of the person may be quite different from the one the counsellor is left with at the end of the assessment session. In some instances, the information the counsellor gathers may place the contents of the referral letter in a different light. For example, a referrer may go to great lengths to discuss the aggressive yet withdrawn and unhelpful behaviour of an individual, and yet you find the client open and pleasant in their dealings with you. Upon further exploration, you discover the client was very angry with the referrer owing to a non-negotiated breach in confidentiality.

However, a referral letter could contain important information and failure to read it might place the counsellor in danger or lead to the client feeling the counsellor has not taken reasonable steps to prepare for their meeting. For example, if a client had been convicted of various violent crimes, it would be sensible to ensure adequate safety precautions are in place for the counsellor. Perhaps the most difficult task for the counsellor is to extract what is pertinent information (such as safety issues) without pre-judging the client.

Basic Administrative Information

A counsellor's first task is to consider what basic information is required for administrative purposes, for example name, address, telephone number (home and work), referral source. In addition, many counsellors take a client's general practitioner's details as part of the initial administrative recording procedure. This latter point may be totally redundant if you are a careers counsellor offering a one-off two hour session regarding retraining or job search. However, if the counsellor is working with clients within a more typical counselling framework, this information could prove crucial in terms of protecting clients and those around them from harm. Counsellors may leave themselves open for claims of negligence if they are not seen to be taking adequate precautions in terms of client safety. A counsellor might find it hard to justify why he or she did not record a client's GP details if called to account in a court of law, as this information could be considered a basic professional requirement (McMahon, 1994).

In many instances, taking the client's date of birth proves useful if the counsellor needs to write to an outside source such as a GP or a psychiatrist. Jungian and transpersonal counsellors with an interest in astrological influences may also want to elicit this information. It is usual practice when contacting someone within the medical profession to give the client's full name, address and date of birth, as this leaves less room for error in securing the correct patient notes. For example:

Dear Dr Jones

re: Miss Julie Martin, 113 Anywhere Street, London, SE3 TL7 DOB: 10 October 1970

It would also be wise to mark the envelope 'private and confidential' as a way of demonstrating commitment to client confidentiality.

Ways of Collating Information

There are many ways in which information can be collated:

■ The counsellor may ask the questions and simply record the answers given.

■ The client may be given a client details form (adapted from McMahon, 1994) to complete (see Figure 2.1).

■ A receptionist or intake worker may record the information prior to the initial assessment session.

■ The counsellor may take the client through a questionnaire and the client completes this either during the first meeting or between the first two meetings.

A written record completed by the client provides more protection for client and counsellor. If such a form is completed (either prior to or at the end of the assessment session) it would be prudent if a paragraph was included which clearly outlined the client's consent to the terms and conditions of the counselling offered (see Figure 2.1). A place for the client's signature and the date would also be helpful, as completion of these by the client is a practical way of demonstrating the client's agreement. This could be of significant benefit if the client ever subsequently denies having been provided with certain information.

Although it is not the purpose of this chapter to discuss preparing the client for counselling, it would be useful to consider how this is to be done as it influences the information sought from the client at this stage. The Palmer and Szymanska (1994) checklist informs clients of the types of questions to ask a counsellor prior to commencing counselling (see Figure 2.2). The checklist is given to clients prior to the assessment interview. Information sheets or brochures covering what is being offered, how it is offered, expectations of client and counsellor (for example, clarity about confidentiality and under what circumstances this will be broken), together with what fees (if any) are to be charged, form part of the information supplied to the client prior to assessment. The client details form is then an administrative follow-on, confirming the client's acceptance and understanding of the counselling being offered and the terms and conditions under which it is offered. Consideration needs to be given to the secure storage of client documentation (such as locked cupboard, filing system), the length of time the information is to be kept after counselling has been completed (for example, 12 months for all details, four years for the client details form only) and how the information is to be disposed of (for example by shredding) (McMahon, 1994). The Data Protection Act 1984 requires those who keep details of individuals on computer to register with the Data Protection Act Registrars.

Client Details Form

General Details

Last Name: _____

First Name: _____

Home Address: _____

_____

_____

Post Code: _____

Telephone Numbers: Home: _____   Work: _____

state full code   *state full code*

General Practitioner's Details:

Doctor's Name: _____

Address: _____

_____

_____

Post Code: _____

Telephone Number: _____

state full code

Client Statement:

I have read and understood all the information supplied to me regarding the terms and conditions under which counselling is being offered and I agree to abide by these. I also give my permission for contact to be made with appropriate external agencies if my counsellor believes I am a danger to myself or to other people.

Signed: _____   **Date:** _____

Figure 2.1   *Client details form*

Issues for the Client to Consider in Counselling or Psychotherapy:

Here is a list of topics or questions you may wish to raise when attending your first counselling (assessment) session:

a) Check that your counsellor has relevant qualifications and experience in the field of counselling/psychotherapy.

b) Ask about the type of approach the counsellor uses and how it relates to your problem.

c) Ask if the counsellor is in supervision (most professional bodies consider supervision to be mandatory; see footnote).

d) Ask whether the counsellor or the counselling agency is a member of a professional body and abides by a code of ethics. If possible, obtain a copy of the code.

e) Discuss your goals/expectations of counselling.

f) Ask about the fees, if any (if your income is low, check if the counsellor operates on a sliding scale) and discuss the frequency and estimated duration of counselling.

g) Arrange regular review sessions with your counsellor to evaluate your progress.

h) Do not enter into a long-term counselling contract unless you are satisfied that this is necessary and beneficial to you.

If you do not have a chance to discuss the above points during your first session, discuss them at the next possible opportunity.

General Issues:

1. Counsellor self-disclosure can sometimes be therapeutically useful. However, if the sessions are dominated by the counsellor discussing his/her own problems at length, raise this issue in the counselling session.

2. If at any time you feel discounted, undermined or manipulated within the session, discuss this with the counsellor. It is easier to resolve issues as and when they arise.

3. Do not accept significant gifts from your counsellor. This does not apply to relevant therapeutic material.

4. Do not accept social invitations from your counsellor. For example, dining in a restaurant or going for a drink. However, this does not apply to relevant therapeutic assignments such as being accompanied by your counsellor into a situation to help you overcome a phobia.

5. If your counsellor proposes a change in venue for the counselling sessions without good reason, do not agree. For example, from a centre to the counsellor's own home.

6. Research has shown that it is not beneficial for clients to have sexual contact with their counsellor. Professional bodies in the field of counselling and psychotherapy consider that it is unethical for counsellors or therapists to engage in sexual activity with current clients.

7. If you have any doubts about the counselling you are receiving then discuss them with your counsellor. If you are still uncertain, seek advice, perhaps from a friend, your doctor, your local Citizens Advice Bureau, the professional body your counsellor belongs to or the counselling agency that may employ your counsellor.

8. You have the right to terminate counselling whenever you choose.

Footnote: Counselling supervision is a formal arrangement where counsellors discuss their counselling in a confidential setting on a regular basis with one or more professional counsellors.

© 1994, Palmer & Szymanska

Figure 2.2 *Issues for client*

Practice Points

Be prepared for your client by reading referral letters.

Be clear about your role in relation to inter-agency liaison.

Ensure your client has received all relevant information relating to the counselling being offered prior to the assessment session.

Have a client details form and any other administrative forms ready when you see the client.

Decide what, if any, written questionnaires form part of the client history-taking process and have these with you when you see the client.

Key Aspects of Client History

Once basic information requirements have been dealt with, the next stage is to consider what other information the counsellor might need from the assessment session and the ways of eliciting this. This next stage helps the counsellor assess the therapeutic needs of his or her client so that an appropriate counselling programme can be developed.

Presenting Problem

Most counsellors, regardless of orientation, start the initial assessment session by asking the client a question such as 'How can I help?' or 'What brings you here?' In most cases, clients then attempt to explain the problems they feel are affecting them. At this stage, the counsellor is gathering information on the presenting problem: what it is, when it started, how it is affecting the client and those around the client, and what forms of self-help the client has tried. Without this information, the counsellor and client might find it hard to move forward and, from the counsellor's perspective, the ability to formulate an appropriate counselling programme is hampered. The client may volunteer the information, in which case the counsellor has only to remember it. Some counsellors take notes during the assessment session both as an aid to memory and as part of their record keeping systems. Others tape the session and use the tape to remind them of relevant details for both client recording and supervision purposes.

Different training schools have different ideas about note-taking during sessions. The majority of person-centred and psychodynamic counsellors see note-taking during a session as a fundamental intrusion into the relationship-building task. They believe this activity detracts from the counsellor's ability to provide total attention to the client. Cognitive-behavioural counsellors tend to believe note-taking is a legitimate part of the helping process. Such note-taking is seen as a way of targeting the needs of the client. Counsellors who work in a more integrative way may advocate a mixture of approaches depending on the needs of the client and the type of information being given, for example no notes being taken when listening to the distress of a recently bereaved person, but quite detailed notes being taken of the ritual behaviour of a person suffering from obsessive compulsive disorder.

Some clients find it difficult to be clear about their problems and the counsellor may find it necessary to ask questions to elicit this information, for example:

> *Client*: I'm not really sure what my problems are or where to start.
>
> *Counsellor*: I imagine it might feel a bit strange talking to someone you have not met before. How about starting wherever you feel most comfortable? Perhaps you could talk about what makes you feel unhappy or discontented, and in what ways you feel your life and those around you are being affected . . . is that OK with you?
>
> *Client*: Yes . . . that's fine with me.

In the process of discussing the presenting problem, the client may speak about many other areas of his or her life, such as: occupation and educational background, family, work and personal relationships (past and present), medical and psychiatric history including medication, previous counselling received and outcome, ethnicity and sexuality, related problems such as anxiety attacks, phobias, problem drinking and eating disorders. This information assists the counsellor to understand the world from the client's perspective and helps the counsellor gain some understanding of the client's current situation. In addition, this information enables the counsellor to make decisions about how best to help the client.

Although not directly related to history taking, it is helpful to ascertain why the client has decided to seek help at this particular time. Gathering such information poses questions about assessment that is covert or counsellor-led as opposed to more self-directed and client-led. This information can provide insight into the client's motivation and the degree of disturbance or distress experienced. A number of possible issues the counsellor may need to consider are as follows (Palmer and Dryden, 1995: 19):

1 Are there signs of 'psychosis'?
2 Are there signs of organicity, organic pathology or any disturbed motor activity?
3 Is there evidence of depression or suicidal or homicidal tendencies?
4 What are the persisting complaints and their main precipitating events?
5 What appear to be some important antecedent factors?
6 Who or what seems to be maintaining the client's overt and covert problems?
7 What does the client wish to derive from counselling or therapy?
8 Are there clear indications or contra-indications for the adoption of a particular therapeutic style, for example is there a preference for a directive or a non-directive style?
9 Are there clear indications as to whether it would be in the client's best interests to be seen individually, as part of a dyad, in a family unit, and/or in a group?
10 Can a mutually satisfying relationship ensue or should the client be referred elsewhere?
11 Has the client previous experience of counselling, therapy or relevant training? If yes, what was the outcome: was the experience positive, negative or neutral, and why?
12 Why is the client seeking counselling/therapy/training at this time and not last week, last month or last year?
13 What are some of the client's positive attributes and strengths?

If a client did not voluntarily provide any additional information over and above the presenting problem, the counsellor would need to consider what subject areas to explore within the assessment session. The following sections cover those areas which are considered the most relevant and common.

Occupational and Educational Background
Details regarding a client's occupation and educational background are helpful. Such information gives the counsellor the opportunity

to assess, for example, intelligence, cognitive processing ability, how active or passive the client is in using opportunities, setbacks and disadvantages experienced, vocational talents and whether these are being used for or against the client. Clients may volunteer this information or the counsellor may pick it out from what the client has said, needing only to check with the client whether the counsellor's understanding is correct. This information helps place the client's current life in context. For example, a client may have excelled within an educational environment, moving easily through university and into a profession, and this information, together with the way in which the client comes across in the assessment session, may help the counsellor recognise how the client uses intellectual powers to rationalise life events. Alternatively, the client may have left school at 16 with no formal qualifications, have been unemployed for years and live in a deprived area. Perhaps by eliciting information about educational establishments the client has attended, the counsellor may discover how isolated the client felt and how educational achievement became a way of coping with this isolation or how lack of educational opportunity has influenced the client's life chances. If the client is still attending college, a student counsellor may be interested in the course the person is taking and feelings about this choice. Additionally, it may be helpful to know if a client has a documented intellectual or cognitive disability: for example, the client may suffer from dyslexia.

Family and Personal Relationships, Past and Present
Very few therapies discount the role relationships play in forming an individual's outlook on the world and the influence childhood has on the way in which people live their lives as adults. Therefore, as far as history taking goes, the type of information required would generally include some details of the client's family of origin. However, as some children are not brought up in a traditional family arrangement, details of significant carers need to be taken. A question such as 'Who did you live with when you were a child?' helps to explore these issues. The question also has the advantage that it is open-ended and makes no assumptions. In addition, history regarding siblings, age ranges, the client's position in the family, whether family members are all living and, if not, the age the client was when they died allows the counsellor to gain some insight into the type of upbringing the client may

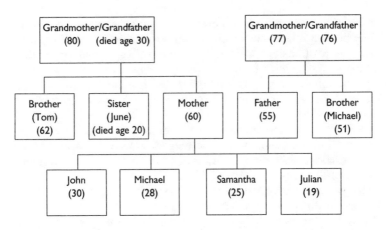

Figure 2.3 *Family tree*

have had and the relationships the client experienced, including how the client felt about those concerned. One of the reasons why counsellors are deemed to need a period of personal therapy is in order to explore personal prejudices. These prejudices could be about other people's backgrounds, cultures, belief systems and relationship styles, and such prejudices could interfere with the counselling process (Syme, 1994; McMahon, 1994).

Psychodynamic and couples counsellors often find information on parents, grandparents and siblings of great value. A family tree is an adaptation of a genogram, the genogram being a tool often used by family therapists to record quite detailed information about an individual's life (Jacobs, 1988). The value of a family tree is that it enables the counsellor and the client to trace particular patterns of events within the family, providing possible insights into the client's situation and feelings (see Figure 2.3).

Information regarding relationships with childhood friends and any other people the client saw as being significant also needs to be included. Such relationships may have had quite a powerful influence on the client's development. For example, a client may have spent most of their childhood with one particular friend and her family, so much so that the client may feel this family is more like her 'real' family than her own biological relatives. In addition, information can be obtained about how these relationships developed, ceased or changed, and what type of relationships the

client has today, including those with work colleagues. The client
may be in a relationship with or without children. Details regarding the relationship such as the type (heterosexual or homosexual), the length of time the couple have been together, the
ages of any children and whether the children are biological,
adopted or stepchildren, all help the counsellor gain a picture of
the client's life.

Some counsellors explore the client's sexuality by eliciting
information about this aspect of their life. Anthony Storr, in the
1979 edition of *The Art of Psychotherapy*, reminds analytic therapists of the importance of taking a full history, including details
relating to sexuality, based on his own early practice and how
failure to do so had a negative impact on his work with clients.
However, counsellors need to be aware that exploring this aspect
may also negatively affect the therapeutic relationship if the client
is unable to see the relevance of the question(s). Clients who have
come to improve their assertiveness in the work setting may feel
questions about their sexuality have no relevance at all. It is
possible the client could perceive the counsellor's questioning
process to be voyeuristic or even abusive.

Medical and Psychiatric History

As counselling is seen more and more as a profession in its own
right, certain expectations and responsibilities are paralleling its
growth. It might be considered negligent of the counsellor to omit
exploration of any past or present medical and/or psychiatric
conditions, including any medication the client may be taking (see
Chapter 3).

In terms of medical conditions, a counsellor does not need to
know about every bout of influenza the client has had. However,
information on illness that may have affected the client's life could
give insight into the client's current psychological state or physical
ability to undertake certain physical tasks in therapy. For example,
physical rage release may not be appropriate for someone with a
back complaint (Stewart, 1989) or heart condition (Palmer and
Dryden, 1995).

In certain types of counselling, such as primal therapy, counsellors routinely elicit information regarding the circumstances of
an individual's birth and details of any early traumas such as
hospitalisation. These details provide crucial information for
assisting the client through experiences such as rebirthing.

It can also be useful to ascertain details of any major physical illnesses or causes of death of parents or siblings as well as any psychiatric problems experienced by family members. Such information may provide a useful insight into issues such as the client's upbringing, life expectancy and fears regarding their own physical or mental health.

A psychiatric label does not rule out counselling as an option. However, the client's current psychological hardiness or predisposition towards certain conditions (e.g. self-harm) needs to be taken into account. Psychological hardiness refers here to the degree of emotional and psychological vulnerability experienced by the client. If a client had a traumatic childhood and later in life suffered occasionally from psychotic episodes, a counsellor would need to consider whether a counselling contract would be of benefit and the type of contact to be made with the client's GP and/or psychiatrist. It may be evident to the counsellor that the client needs to explore his or her early childhood experiences and yet equally evident that to do so could lead to a psychological breakdown at the current time.

Previous Counselling Outcomes

Details regarding previous counselling or psychotherapeutic intervention provide useful insights into the client's motivation and progress to date. Therefore, information regarding the type of counselling received, duration and outcome can be usefully elicited by the counsellor. An initial question such as 'Have you ever had any previous counselling help before coming to see me?' is sufficient. Such information enables the counsellor to assess whether the form of counselling on offer is likely to be effective or not. For example, a client may have seen a succession of counsellors of varying orientations for a particular problem over an extended period. If this were the case, the current counsellor would need to consider what, if anything, could be offered that had not been offered by the other counsellors. The client may also have received counselling support from other professionals such as social workers and health visitors.

However, even if a client has had counselling it does not automatically follow that the counsellor cannot be of assistance. For example, clients are not always ready for change, or the quality of the counselling received may have been questionable, or they may have experienced only one type of counselling. The current counsellor may be 'in the right place at the right time' to effect client change and be able to offer a more appropriate type of help for the client's problem. A realistic rather than a pessimistic or an optimistic attitude is required.

Ethnicity, Sexuality and Disability

Details about sexuality and ethnicity are helpful as they provide insight into the client's cultural belief systems, including any prejudice and discrimination experienced. Such details also need to take into account the client's country of origin, their religion and the reasons why the client is residing in this country, for example out of choice or owing to persecution which has led to refugee status. Some forms of counselling do not take into account the effect of the society the person lives in, believing that any difficulties experienced are more about the client's inner rather than outer world. However, increasingly more weight is being given to the effects of social environment and the interplay between the external and internal world of the client. Social class may also influence a client's experiences, as will the generation the client was born into, and these two additional points require consideration. Details regarding a client's disability also need to be considered as the client may have experienced personal difficulties and prejudice within society. Recognition of the importance of social context is given by the British Association for Counselling in its *Code of Ethics and Practice for Counsellors*, which states: 'Counsellors will take all reasonable steps to take account of the client's social context' (1993: 2.7.3).

Client Goals

Although this chapter is about history taking, it would be remiss to omit the need to elicit clear client goals (see Chapters 6–8). Client goals do not necessarily have to be as specific as those sought by cognitive-behavioural or solution-focused counsellors. A client may state a specific goal, such as 'I do not want to experience panic attacks when giving presentations.' However, another client may want to use counselling 'to explore my feelings about my childhood' or 'just to have someone to talk to'. It is important that both the client and the counsellor are clear about the goals they are working towards so they can measure progress through whatever therapeutic method is chosen. Clients may have been partially successful in working towards their stated goals. Therefore, information regarding their achievements, failures and disappointments will also prove useful.

Related Problems

Unlike the other areas previously mentioned, there is one part of the history-taking process which is more variable. Some counsellors are content to let anything else over and above the subject areas already mentioned arise as the counselling proceeds, whilst others pursue additional structured information gathering exercises. They may choose to do so either because of their own therapeutic orientation or because of the client's presenting problem. For example, a stress counsellor may want information about caffeine intake, alcohol and other drug consumption, exercise, diet, and rest and relaxation periods and activities, amongst other lifestyle information, and will see this information as essential and therefore to be sought from every client seen. A psychodynamic counsellor may wish for fuller details about the client's feelings regarding close family. A debt counsellor helping a client explore financial difficulties may want to focus on those issues. A careers counsellor may want a much more detailed breakdown of the client's occupational and educational history.

Practice Points

You need to decide which topic areas are essential in the client history-taking process and which are of a more discretionary nature depending on the client's individual problem, for example debt.

You need to consider what information regarding social context is to be sought. Particular attention needs to be paid to issues surrounding ethnicity, sexuality and disability.

Level of Detail Required

One method of obtaining detailed information is by using the Multimodal Life History Inventory (Lazarus and Lazarus, 1991; see Appendix). This is completed by the client and elicits information regarding all aspects of a client's life. It is currently 15 pages long and covers seven subject areas (or modalities as they are called): behaviours, feelings, physical sensations, mental images, thoughts, interpersonal relationships and biological details. Multimodal counsellors stress the importance of having as much information as possible from which to develop appropriate therapeutic and counselling programmes targeted at the specific needs of the client (see Chapter 7).

Person-centred and psychodynamic counsellors may experience a less favourable reaction to gathering such detailed information as they may believe this 'gets in the way' of their primary task of relationship building. Although not all cognitive-behavioural counsellors would want the type of detailed information required by the Multimodal Life History Inventory, there would not be the same aversion to the idea of gathering information as with some other therapeutic orientations.

Methods of Eliciting Information

The next stage in the process is to consider what methods the counsellor is going to use to elicit relevant information. A counsellor could gather as much information as possible via a questionnaire given to the client prior to the initial assessment session. Some counsellors prefer to have a short first meeting where the method of working is outlined, a questionnaire is presented and the client is asked to return the completed questionnaire prior to the next session. Other counsellors prefer to have certain questions in written form and rely on the assessment session to elicit the remainder verbally. Other forms of eliciting information include collecting data in a diagrammatic form favoured by cognitive-analytic therapists (Ryle, 1995), using lifelines completed by the client (see Figure 2.4) and writing a life story.

The use of questionnaires in the assessment process is perhaps more popular amongst clinical psychologists and cognitive-behavioural psychotherapists than amongst counsellors. Some counsellors do not use questionnaires but rely on a well proven structure recalled from memory which elicits the same information as the questionnaire, the counsellor recording this information at the end of the assessment session. The counsellor needs to ensure consistency in application regardless of variations in mood (self or client) which could lead to parts of the structure being missed out. This is less likely to happen where a questionnaire or written assessment is used. It is important to remember that the client may not wish to answer any or all of the questions asked, regardless of how the counsellor attempts to elicit answers.

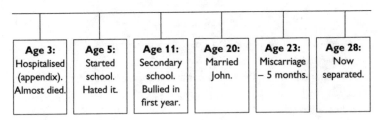

Figure 2.4 *Lifeline*

Many counsellors feel that questionnaires are cold and impersonal and that asking too many questions at the assessment session detracts from the task of relationship building. However, questionnaires can also be perceived by clients as a helpful way of structuring their thoughts and engendering a sense of confidence in the counselling process. Additionally, how the questionnaire is introduced to the client will greatly affect the client's attitude and feelings about its completion. An impersonal 'complete this' followed by a lengthy questionnaire could be seen as cold and impersonal.

However, if the questionnaire is introduced as a means for the counsellor to help the client in the most appropriate way, the client is more likely to see it as a friendly tool. Counselling and relationship-building skills can also be used when introducing a questionnaire to a client. Additionally, clients can be reassured that they do not have to answer any questions they are unhappy or unsure about and that these can be discussed with the counsellor later. The counsellor also needs to be sure that the client's literacy level is up to the task in hand as some clients are embarrassed to admit problems in this area. The client may, for example, suffer from dyslexia or may have a physical problem which makes completing the form difficult. One of my colleagues completed a form on behalf of a client as the client was suffering from repetitive strain injury (RSI) and could not do it himself.

Perhaps what is more important is the consistency of information gathering by the counsellor. Failure to adhere to any consistent client history-taking style means that a rather *ad hoc* form of client assessment takes place. Whatever the orientation of the counsellor, the client care and the quality control aspects of the assessment process can be hampered by *ad hoc* approaches.

Practice Points

Decide how you are going to collect your information (written or verbally).

Consider how you will ensure a consistent approach for each client.

Do not make any assumptions about a client's ability to complete written information.

Conclusion

This chapter has explored a variety of subject areas for consideration when taking a client history. The reader can select some or all of what has been said to enhance the assessment process with clients. A structured client history-taking process can be built into the armoury of methods used by counsellors who, with experience, will be able to develop the model believed to be of greatest benefit.

References

British Association for Counselling (1993) *Code of Ethics and Practice for Counsellors*. Rugby: BAC.

Jacobs, M. (1988) *Psychodynamic Counselling in Action*. London: Sage.

Lazarus, A.A. and Lazarus, C.N. (1991) *Multimodal Life History Inventory*. Champaign, IL: Research Press.

McMahon, G. (1994) *Starting Your Own Private Practice*. Cambridge: National Extension College.

Palmer, S. and Dryden, W. (1995) *Counselling for Stress Problems*. London: Sage.

Palmer, S. and Szymanska, K. (1994) 'Referral guidance for participants attending stress management training courses', *Stress News*, 5(4): 11.

Ryle, A. (1995) *Cognitive Analytic Therapy*. Chichester: Wiley.

Stewart, I. (1989) *Transactional Analysis Counselling in Action*. London: Sage.

Storr, A. (1979) *The Art of Psychotherapy*. London: Secker & Warburg and Heinemann.

Syme, G. (1994) *Counselling in Independent Practice*. Buckingham: Open University Press.

3 Medical and Psychiatric Assessment

Berni Curwen

Much of the material discussed in this chapter may be unfamiliar to counsellors unless they also have prior training in fields such as psychiatry or social work. It is important that counsellors do not attempt to practise outside their realms of competence. For example the majority of counsellors would not undertake a comprehensive mental state examination but a knowledge of the process may widen their understanding (see Lukas, 1993; Morrison, 1995). Some of the procedures outlined below may already have been carried out by another professional when an agency refers an individual to you.

Information Gathering: the Benefits of Medical and Psychiatric Assessment

Wherever possible you will gain a better overall picture from a client if you can supplement it with information from a close relative or another person. Clients are sometimes unaware of the extent to which their symptoms affect them. A history is best recorded systematically and in a logical, predetermined order. It is not always possible to gather information in the same order with every client. Flexibility is required to enable the client not to feel unduly restricted by the interviewer. It is better to be open about what you record of session(s) with your client. Open discussion at the beginning of assessment is usually preferable. Explain that you

Table 3.1 *Main points of history taking*

Circumstances of the interview	Marital history
Account of present problems	Past medical/surgical history
Family history	Past psychiatric history
Personal history	Present life situation
Menstrual history	Personality
Sexual history	Information check

need to record relevant information to help ensure that important themes are not overlooked, and that the information is a means of reflecting back and monitoring progress through supervision. If the information recorded is to be seen by anyone other than your counselling supervisor – and this may happen in certain circumstances, for example in the National Health Service – this would usually be discussed with your client and take place with his or her agreement. There may be exceptional cases where this is not possible, and these will need to be discussed with your counselling supervisor.

I will reiterate briefly what needs to be covered in the history-taking assessment. This will serve as a checklist for the beginner and a reminder for the more experienced interviewer of the topics which make up a complete history. It is neither necessary nor possible to ask every question of every client. Common sense needs to be used in judging how each topic should be explored with particular clients. You will learn as a trainee how to adjust your questioning to problems that emerge as the interview proceeds (Leff and Isaacs, 1990).

As history taking within clinical practice has been discussed in Chapter 2, I will merely present this material as Table 3.1. History assessment is an important facet of information gathering.

You may gain information from many different agencies during the course of interviewing your client. If other agencies are involved, and with the consent of your client, it may be beneficial to obtain their assessments or reports, for example from a general practitioner, community mental health nurse, social worker or psychiatric specialist. This information will be most vital where a client has a history of violence, or is extremely disturbed. If this were the case he would ideally not be seen alone. Be sure to make your organisation aware of the situation and adhere to the policies and guidelines for dealing with clients with this element of risk. Where your organisation has no policies in place concerning counsellor safety, it will be all the more necessary for you to bear safety aspects in mind. It is inadvisable to be in the building alone; make colleagues aware that you are assessing a potentially disturbed or aggressive person. It is also helpful to familiarise yourself with physical means of protection, such as emergency exits and panic alarms.

This additional information from others may provide a different perspective, for example, enabling you to pinpoint the date of onset, especially when the client experiences difficulty in remembering. This is usually the case if illness was gradual. When this type of information is given by a third party it will be treated in confidence, subject to any limits suggested by your code of ethics (see Chapter 1), which are best discussed with the information-giver.

Agency collaboration is important when dealing with potentially violent or aggressive clients. Where there is previous information, read it. (Some counsellors, for example person-centred, often object to this practice.) This may help you to decide if there is risk of violence or of suicide. Reading these notes may help you to evaluate the risk to you, others or the client. If you have access to other professionals' information about the client, keep in mind that this might now be inaccurate for two reasons. First, it refers to an earlier time in the client's life and may not necessarily apply now: always be sure to check the date. Second, referral letters may give relevant information and also give an indication of what a particular client's problems may be. Again bear in mind as you assess the client yourself that the referral may have been inaccurate in the first instance.

The motivation of the client is important (see Chapter 4). There may be a marked difference in the effectiveness of counselling depending on whether the client sought referral himself or was forced into it, for example 'My wife said she would leave me if I did not get help for my gambling.' The client's experience of therapy in the past may determine his attitudes towards the success or failure of counselling. If, for whatever reason, it did not work in the past, it is useful to find out why not. It is also important to find out why he is coming for treatment at this time. When assessing a client's motivation, remain aware that psychiatric illness, such as severe depression, may be a contributing factor towards lack of motivation.

Table 3.2 *Essential areas of mental state examination*

Appearance and behaviour
Speech
Mood
Depersonalisation and derealisation
Obsessional traits
Delusions
Hallucinations and illusions
Orientation
Attention and concentration
Memory
Insight

Mental State Examination

An integral part of a thoroughgoing assessment is the mental state examination. During the course of your history taking you will have observed and noted the client's symptoms up to the time of the actual mental state examination. The mental state examination is concerned with the symptoms and behaviour at the time of the interview. There is a degree of overlap between the history and the mental state, mainly in observations about mood, delusions and hallucinations. A good counsellor is a good observer.

As noted above, another means of assessing behaviour is from accounts of others who are involved, such as parents, a spouse or other professionals. During the interview you will observe only a small sample of the client's behaviour. Accounts from others may be more revealing. This is worth bearing in mind.

The purpose of a mental state examination is to detect abnormal features in a client's state of mind, and behaviour, at the time of the assessment (Table 3.2). If abnormal features are found, this information contributes to the diagnostic process. Carrying out a mental state examination may at first seem a laborious task but is a practical skill that can be learnt by watching experienced interviewers and by practising under supervision (Leff and Isaacs, 1990; Wing et al., 1974). Observations of interpersonal dynamics are also important when interviewing a family or a couple. The family or couple will interact during the interview, and this may give important clues to both the contributing causes of the problem and the most appropriate help (see Chapter 4).

Appearance and Behaviour

The client's appearance and behaviour need careful observation. Ask yourself what you noticed first about the client. Did he look healthy or sick? Did he look dirty or unkempt? This may indicate self-neglect or several other possibilities including alcoholism, drug addiction, depression, dementia or schizophrenia.

Note the client's body build. An appearance suggesting recent weight loss may indicate the possibility of physical illness, anorexia nervosa, depressive disorder or anxiety neurosis.

You may observe your client wearing bright colours and adopting incongruous styles of dress. This could possibly lead you to consider psychosis or schizophrenia. A client keeping their coat on during a boiling hot day may be evidence of a belief of being taken over by aliens from another planet or a sign of poverty and inability to afford a summer coat. Rather than infer from a single observation you should use this to point towards further assessment: for example, wearing bright colours and adopting incongruous styles of dress might suggest colour-blindness rather than schizophrenia. It is the overall pattern and extent of symptoms which are necessary to guide your judgement (see Chapter 1).

Facial Expression

Information about mood can be observed via facial expression. In depression a common characteristic is the turning down of the corners of the mouth, and vertical furrows on the brow. In anxious clients there may be raised eyebrows and dilated (enlarged) pupils. Your client may exhibit a whole range of emotions through facial expression including elation, irritability and anger, together with the mask-like expression of clients taking drugs with parkinsonism side-effects.

Posture and Movement

Posture and movement also reflect mood. You will observe that a depressed client will usually sit leaning forwards with their shoulders hunched and their head inclined downwards, gazing at the floor. An anxious client may be observed perched on the edge of a chair, head held erect, and often with hands gripping the side of the chair. Clients with an agitated depression, as with anxiety, may exhibit shakiness and restlessness, for example touching jewellery or rearranging clothes. Clients with mania may be observed to be overactive and restless.

Social Behaviour

A client with schizophrenia may behave unusually. They may be overactive and socially disinhibited or withdrawn and preoccupied; others may be aggressive. Clients with antisocial personality disorders may also appear aggressive. When you record this behaviour you should give a clear description of what the client actually does. Do not use subjective terms such as 'bizarre', but use descriptive terms such as 'completely covers face with jumper'.

Speech

It is important to record both how the client speaks and what he says. Usually fast speech may indicate mania or slow speech may indicate depressive disorders. The amount of speech is increased in some clients, such as clients who are anxious. Clients suffering from depression or dementia may pause for a long time before replying to questions and have little spontaneity of speech: tone may be monotonous and they may be hesitant and easily distracted. Sudden interruptions may indicate thought blocking but are more often effects of distraction. Rapid shifts from one subject to another may suggest flight of ideas.

A characteristic of schizophrenia is that of thought disorder: a lack of logical thread and general diffuseness may indicate this. Neologisms are a characteristic of schizophrenia and are private words often used to describe personal experiences.

Mood

Assess your client's mood by combining observations of behaviour and appearance, particularly facial expression and posture, with what the client tells you about how he feels. If low mood is detected, enquire about feeling tearful, thoughts of pessimism about the future, hopelessness about the future and guilt about the past. Do not be afraid to ask open questions about suicidal ideation but be sensitive in your enquiry. (We shall explore this in much more detail in the section about suicide.) It will be helpful to find out if your client is generally cheerful or gloomy, whether he has marked changes in mood, and if so how quickly they appear, how long they last and if they follow life events.

Anxiety

When you are assessing anxiety you need to ask about physical symptoms and the thoughts which accompany them. A question such as 'What goes through your mind when you feel anxious?' will enable you to detect anxious thoughts and may lead to the client responding by telling you about their thoughts and fears of fainting or of losing control or 'going mad'.

Depersonalisation and Derealisation

These may be difficult to assess and clients may have difficulty describing their experiences. An example of a question to ask here would be, 'Do you ever feel that things around you are unreal?' It is also useful to gain examples of your client's experiences. A client with depersonalisation may describe herself as being detached from her surroundings or unable to feel emotion. A client with derealisation often describes things as seeming 'artificial' and 'lifeless' in his own environment.

Obsessional Aspects

The terms 'obsession' and 'compulsion' are closely associated but do not mean the same. A continuous experience of an unwanted thought is known as an obsession. A compulsion is always a deed. Clients can be ashamed of their obsessional thoughts especially those with violent or sexual themes. Your client may report to you that he is experiencing a thought over and over again that he does not understand and wishes it would go away, but cannot stop himself thinking no matter what he does. You will need to ask your client for examples of what thoughts keep coming into his mind, to enable you to establish the theme.

Compulsions can be observed but are more often performed unobtrusively. Clients will often be embarrassed or humiliated when telling you about their compulsions. They may tell you that they know what they are doing is 'crazy or silly' but they must do it and cannot stop themselves. Your client may tell you about rituals. Explore these fully. They may lead you to establish that it takes your client an hour to wash his hands because he has to repeat the action many times in exactly the same way. Most compulsions cluster around one of three types of actions: counting, repetitive cleaning or washing, and checking.

Delusions

Clients can skilfully hide delusions. An example may be that of a persecutory delusion where an individual may believe others are attempting to inflict harm upon him. You will need to be alert to evasions. If you discover a delusion is held you need to ascertain how strongly held this belief is. You should not argue with a client about his delusion but sometimes you will need to test out the strength of his belief. Use an inquiring manner, try not to antagonise him and do not become argumentative. If the client is from a different culture from you, be alert and aware that his beliefs may be culturally determined (Rack, 1982). It will be useful to find out if his belief would be shared by others from a similar background. Some delusions are more difficult to recognise than others and tend to be specific: delusions of control where a client may believe that someone or something is controlling what he does, says or thinks, or what he can do to others (Schneider, 1949). Others that are specific are ideas of reference where a client believes that significant or unrelated events in the world have a secret meaning aimed at him. There are delusions of persecution (see Freud, 1911), for example where a client may tell you he is being followed by the woman who sold him his lottery ticket last week.

Illusions and Hallucinations
When assessing for illusions and hallucinations you need to be clear of the difference. Illusions refer to sensory events that are misperceived, such as a hat stand in the darkened corner of your office which your client tells you he sees as a gangster wearing a hat. If the client is convinced of this fact it is an illusion. The client may report an experience of the five senses – sight, smell, taste, touch and hearing. If this is unrelated to any external stimuli, and clearly not true, this is a hallucination. You will need to be tactful when making enquiries regarding hallucinations. Some clients may think you regard them as 'mad'. It will be helpful to say something like, 'Some people have unusual experiences when their nerves are upset.' The client may be more prepared to elaborate and say he has seen an angel beckoning to him (a visual hallucination) or hears his dead mother's voice talking to him (an auditory hallucination) or smells rotting fish (an olfactory hallucination). A tactile hallucination, where the client believes he is being touched or has insects crawling under his skin, is more unusual, as is a gustatory hallucination where a client may believe that he tastes poison.

Orientation

What you will need to assess is the client's orientation of time, place and person. You will have become aware of the client's orientation throughout the process of the assessment and may not need to ask specific questions at this stage. To assess time orientation you can ask about the current day, month or year. To assess orientation of place you can enquire about where the client thinks he is and how he got there. To assess orientation of person the client may be asked questions about his spouse or children and what their relationship is to him. You need to remember that healthy people do not always know the exact date or day of the week.

Concentration and Attention

You will be assessing whether your client can pay attention to what you are discussing. As with orientation this may have become evident to the assessor during other stages of the interview. But if in doubt formal tests may add to this information. It is usual to ask the client to subtract 7 from 100 and then to take 7 from the remainder repeatedly (Rose, 1994: 35). However, errors may be due to lack of skill in arithmetic. If poor performance is due to this then you may ask the client to recite the months of the year in reverse order.

Memory

There are three spheres of memory to be assessed: immediate memory, recent memory and remote memory. It will be helpful to assess these along with other information gathered about the client's ability to remember. When there are doubts regarding an individual's ability to remember, your assessment may be supplemented with standardised psychological tests. These provide quantative assessment of the progression of potential memory disorder (Wechsler, 1945).

Your client's immediate memory may be assessed by asking him to repeat sequences of digits that have been spoken slowly enough for him to reasonably register them. A normal response of a person of average intelligence is that they are able to repeat back seven digits correctly. Recent memory is assessed by asking about news items from the last day or two, or asking about events in the client's life which are known to the interviewer or about what the client did yesterday. Remote memory is assessed by asking the client what town he lived in as a 12 year old and names of earlier political leaders.

When assessing elderly people, standardised ratings of memory for recent personal events, past personal events and general events help to distinguish between people with cerebral pathology and those without (Post, 1965).

Insight

Insight refers to whether or not the client thinks he has a problem. At this stage of the mental state examination the assessor will have a good idea of how far the client is aware of the state of his health. Direct questions can be asked to ascertain his awareness of the illness, for example 'Do you think there is anything the matter with you?' If he does, you next need to know if he wishes to have help for himself. If so, why now? You are attempting to ascertain whether or not his perception of his problem is reasonably accurate. For example, a person with a problematic relationship might unrealistically attribute all problems to his partner, whereas another person in a similar situation might recognise, and wish to deal with, their own input to the problem. The answers to these questions are important because they determine in part whether the client is suitable for therapy.

Summary

If you see or hear anything which makes you feel endangered, or if the client is out of touch with reality or might hurt himself or someone else, there are appropriate steps that you can take to reassure yourself and the client. Assessing a client for risk of suicide is discussed later in this chapter. By following a structured approach and by asking both open and closed questions, as well as using your powers of observation and making written descriptions of behaviours, you will be enabled by the mental state examination to:

1   gain information about the client and their emotional difficulties in the here and now as well as in the past
2   determine their suitability for treatment or for further referral to the appropriate agency when necessary
3   assess the client's current mental state and/or ongoing mental health problems

4   identify significant risk factors
5   use the information gained to develop client-led treatment
     programmes (Institute of Psychiatry, 1973; Appleby and
     Forshaw, 1990).

Practice Points

Remain aware of your own safety as well as that of your client.

Information about your client is confidential. You may need to go outside the realms of the confidential relationship to prevent suicidal ideation becoming a reality, or for the safety of yourself and others.

A good counsellor is a good observer.

It is important that counsellors do not attempt to practise outside the realms of their competence.

The mental state examination is concerned with the symptoms and behaviour of the client at the time of the interview.

The mental state examination is an aid to diagnosis.

Flexibility is required to enable the client not to feel unduly restricted by the interviewer.

Use descriptive terms of what the client actually does, not subjective terms such as 'bizarre'.

Listen to how the client speaks and to what he says.

Diagnosis and the Use of Statistical Manuals

There are two widely accepted classifications of psychiatric disorders: the *International Classification of Diseases* (ICD 10), published by the World Health Organisation (1992), and the American Psychiatric Association's (1994) *Diagnostic and Statistical Manual of Mental Disorders* (fourth edition, DSM IV). The classifications are broadly similar, and the people involved in preparing them have worked closely together, producing codes and terms which are fully compatible.

All branches of medicine operate a disease classification. In psychiatry diagnostic labels are more often defined by clusters of symptoms or clinical features. Diagnosis will enable the clinician first to describe and secondly to summarise the client's condition, which allows rational decisions to be made about treatment and other aspects of clinical management. Before a diagnosis can be made a great deal of information is required. Hence the importance of information gathering. Diagnosis also implies understanding patterns of an illness, suggesting a specific treatment and an expected outcome or prognosis. We diagnose mental disorders in an attempt to communicate reliably and effectively with one another about a client's problems. A diagnosis enables you to clearly and concisely define an individual's problems in a way that will be recognised by other clinicians, including doctors.

Counsellors should be aware of the major psychiatric disorders outlined in Table 3.3. Certain conditions may make counselling difficult, such as counselling somebody who is actively suicidal or dealing with somebody who is diagnosed as suffering from schizophrenia, and actively hallucinating. Recent research suggests that cognitive-behavioural therapy may be useful when clients experience hallucinations and delusions (Kingdom and Turkington, 1994).

Practice Points

There are two widely accepted classifications of psychiatric disorder.

A diagnosis allows rational decisions to be made about treatment and other aspects of clinical management.

Clinicians will benefit from a knowledge of the major psychiatric disorders.

A diagnosis matches signs and symptoms, of sufficient intensity and duration, against a known category of disorder.

Suicide

As a counsellor you will almost certainly have encountered clients who say they wish to take their own life. You may already have experienced the confusion of feelings surrounding that of a friend, relative, or acquaintance who has already committed suicide. The fact is that any person who wants to end his own life may find a way to do so. This section is about how to explore and how to assess for suicidal ideation and suicidal potential.

Table 3.3 *Major categories of psychiatric disorder*

Mood disorders

Major depressive disorder	One or more depressive episodes, that is two weeks of depressed mood and loss of interest
Dysthymic disorder	Two years of predominantly depressed mood not continuous and depressed symptoms not as severe as above
Depressive disorder not otherwise specified	Does not reach criteria for major depressive disorder, or others as above
Bipolar I disorder	One or more manic or mixed episodes often with depressive episode(s)
Bipolar II disorder	One or more major depressive episodes with one or more hypomanic episode(s)
Cyclothymic disorder	Hypomanic symptoms for two years and numerous episodes of depressive symptoms
Bipolar disorder not otherwise specified	Bipolar features not meeting criteria for any specific bipolar disorder
Mood disorder due to general medical condition	Disturbance in mood directly physiologically linked to general medical condition
Substance-induced mood disorder	Disturbance in mood directly physiologically linked to a drug of abuse; medication or toxin exposure
Mood disorder not otherwise specified	Mood symptoms not a specified mood disorder nor depressive disorder or bipolar disorder

Anxiety disorders

Panic attack	Sudden intense fear; apprehension; fearfulness and terror. During attack: shortness of breath; palpitations; chest pain and choking sensation; fear of losing control
Agoraphobia	Avoidance of situations or places
Panic disorder without agoraphobia	Recurrent panic attacks with persistent concern
Panic disorder with agoraphobia	Recurrent panic attacks and agoraphobia
Agoraphobia without history of panic attacks	Agoraphobia; panic-like symptoms, no real unexpected panic attacks
Specific phobia	Anxiety; feared object/situation avoidance behaviour
Social phobia	Anxiety with social performance avoidance behaviour
Obsessive compulsive disorder	Obsessions and/or compulsions
Post-traumatic stress disorder	Re-experiencing of traumatic event; increased arousal; avoidance of reminders of trauma; diagnosis after one month

continued overleaf

Table 3.3 *(continued)*

Acute stress disorder	Occurring immediately following extreme traumatic event
Generalised anxiety disorder	Six months of panic and worry
Anxiety disorder due to a general medical condition	Anxiety symptoms physiological consequence of general medical condition
Substance-induced anxiety disorder	Anxiety symptoms physiological consequence of a drug of abuse; medication or toxin exposure
Anxiety disorder not otherwise specified	Anxiety or phobic avoidance where the criteria do not meet the above
Personality disorders	
Paranoid personality disorder	Distrust, suspiciousness
Schizoid personality disorder	Social detachment, restricted emotional expression
Schizotypal personality disorder	Discomfort of close relationships, behavioural eccentricities, perceptual distortions
Antisocial personality disorder	Disregard, violation of others' rights
Borderline personality disorder	Impulsive, instability in interpersonal relationships
Histrionic personality disorder	Lively, dramatic, attention seeking, emotional excitability
Narcissistic personality disorder	Grandiose sense of self-importance, lacks empathy, needs admiration
Avoidant personality disorder	Social inhibition, feelings of inadequacy, hypersensitivity
Dependent personality disorder	Submissive, clinging
Obsessive personality disorder	Orderliness, perfectionism, control
Personality disorder not otherwise specified	Traits for personality disorder but none specific
Eating disorders	
Anorexia nervosa	Refusal to maintain minimum body weight, refusal of food, distorted perception of shape, size or body. Afraid of weight gain, amenorrhoea (absence of menstruation)
Bulimia nervosa	Binge eating, self-induced vomiting, misuse of laxatives, diuretics, fasting, excessive exercise
Schizophrenia/psychotic disorders	
Schizophrenia	Delusions or hallucinations, disorganised speech, disorganised behaviour, catatonic behaviour

continued

Table 3.3 *(continued)*

Schizophreniform	Symptoms equivalent to schizophrenia disturbance, one to six months' decline in functioning
Schizoaffective disorder	Disturbance of mood, delusions, hallucinations
Delusional disorder	Non-bizarre delusions
Brief psychotic disorder	Psychotic disturbance lasting more than a day, less than one month
Shared psychotic disorder	Influenced by another who already has a delusion
Psychotic disorder due to general medical condition	Psychotic symptoms physiologically linked to general medical condition
Substance-induced psychotic disorder	Physiologically linked to drug abuse, medication or toxin exposure
Sleep disorders	
Primary sleep disorders	Dyssomnias: difficulty initiating sleep or maintaining sleep, narcolepsy, breathing-related sleep disorders Parasomnias: abnormal behaviour or physiological events, such as nightmares, sleep walking
Sleep disorder related to another mental disorder	Related to mental disorder, such as mood or anxiety
Sleep disorder related to general medical condition	Direct physiological effects
Substance-induced sleep disorder	Disturbance in sleep severe, direct effect of a drug of abuse, medication, toxin

In England and Wales suicide verdicts are decided by coroners, who require: first, evidence that the act was self-inflicted; and secondly, evidence that the death was intended, for example a suicide note. Official suicide statistics underestimate the true suicide rate. Many suicides go unrecorded because 'accidental death' or 'undetermined cause' will be recorded by the coroner.

Suicide is more common in men than women, and is usually rare under the age of 14 (Shaffer, 1974). Risk of suicide increases with age, peaking in women in their late 50s and in men in their late 60s. Suicide has increased in young men aged 25 to 35 and decreased in older people of both sexes aged 45 to 65.

There are well established factors for those who are at risk of suicide, as in Table 3.4, with men being at greater risk than women.

Table 3.4   *Those at risk for suicide*

Male	Previous suicide attempts
Single, widowed, divorced	Social isolation
Older (less risk than used to be)	Life-threatening or chronic physical illness
Psychiatric illness, depression,	Unemployment
alcohol/drug abuse, schizophrenia	

Methods Used for Suicide

People use many different methods to commit suicide. Drug overdoses account for about two-thirds of suicides amongst women and a third in men. The drugs commonly used are the analgesics and antidepressants. The most common methods used by males for suicide are car exhaust poisoning and hanging. Males tend to use acts of violence more than women. Shooting is another form of suicide used by males but is much more common in the United States where firearms are readily available. The remaining deaths in England and Wales are by a variety of physical means: jumping from high places, falling in front of moving vehicles or trains (Symonds, 1985).

Some countries have a higher incidence of successful suicide than others, Japan being amongst the highest. Suicide is culturally prominent in Japan (Retterstol, 1993).

Antecedents of Suicide

The majority of suicides have a psychiatric disorder, with depression, schizophrenia, drug addiction and alcohol addiction as the main diagnoses found among suicide victims. Other risk factors for suicide include social problems, personality disorders, physical illness and life events (Table 3.5).

In recent years great consideration has been given to genetic and biological risk factors for suicide in depressive disorders (Roy, 1992; 1982). Research into life events, stress and illness shows that problems occur in both mental and physical health (Heikkinen et al., 1994). People with AIDS have 66 times higher suicide rates than the general population (Marzuk et al., 1988). Prior to committing suicide a vast majority of people have made their intentions known to at least one other person, often more (Robins et al., 1959).

Table 3.5 *Antecedents of suicide*

Psychiatric	Social	Physical
Depression	Isolation	Terminal Illness
Hopelessness	Withdrawal	AIDS
Helplessness	Bereavement	Dementia
Ambivalence	Separation	Huntington's chorea
Post-trauma stress	Loss	Neurological disorders
Alcohol addiction	No family support	Cancer
Drug addiction	Financial problems	Stroke
Schizophrenia	Domestic factors	
Personality disorder	Unemployment	
	Alienation from peers	

Suicidal Ideation

It is not unusual for 'normal' individuals to experience occasional suicidal thoughts. In clinical assessment if your client is talking of suicide you will need to take this seriously. Your client may convey these messages in various ways such as in behaviour, writing, pictures or verbally. Asking a client about suicidal ideation does not make suicidal behaviour more likely: the contrary is true. This open discussion and frankness will enable the client to feel understood and less alienated. It is important for you to assess whether your client is entertaining suicidal ideas at the present time. Use open questions such as 'How do you feel about the future?' The client's response may be verbal and indirect, for example 'I wish I could go to sleep and never have to wake up', or more direct: 'I wish I was dead.' Be aware of the non-verbal indications that your client is suicidal such as the giving away of personal possessions, or a tidying-up of personal affairs. Cessation of eating or drinking or both may be other non-verbal indications of suicide. You should be alert to any expressions of hopelessness, helplessness or pessimism about the client's situation or the chances of recovery. As discussed earlier, if you have access to previous notes, pay attention to the mental state examination. This will enable you to ascertain if your client has told someone before that she was thinking of hurting herself. If your client has made an attempt on her life previously, whether dangerous or token, this is an important predictor that she may contemplate suicide in the future. Suicide and parasuicide (attempted suicide) were seen as a single problem before 1950 (Stengel, 1952) until Stengel distinguished between the two forms of behaviour (1952). These ideas were further developed a few years later (Stengel and Cook, 1958).

Warning Signs

Reading through your client's history it is helpful to be aware of warning signs. One is that your client has a history of substance misuse: drugs and alcohol can prevent your client from thinking logically. A second is a family history of suicide, which may indicate familiarity with suicide as a problem-solving technique. Once you have established and entered into discussion and dialogue about suicidal ideation, remember to make detailed notes for you and others to refer to, if necessary, at a later date.

You will now need to ask questions about the suicide plan, method and intended outcome to determine lethality, or the potential to cause death. An example of a question here might be 'Have you made any plans about hurting yourself or thought about how you might go about it?' If you get a response which shows the client has no plans, he may answer 'I have not thought about it to that extent.' If this is the case, allow your client to explore his thoughts and feelings within that safe environment. If you get a response which indicates a specific method has been considered, for example 'I think about jumping in front of the tube train', you will need to find out when your client last experienced thoughts of harming herself and how often these thoughts occur. Ask her about the intensity of these thoughts and whether they interfere with her life. Before an act of suicide, a client may become more comfortable with the thought of dying and communicate no fear; she may communicate that death is seen as a happy release from suffering or as an opportunity for reunion with a dead parent or spouse.

A precise plan with a lethal method arranged for the next 24 to 48 hours constitutes a high risk. I would suggest immediate intervention with hospitalisation. Supervision is required to prevent a suicide attempt by high risk clients. This level of supervision may depend upon the setting in which you work. You may be able to arrange for a psychiatric assessment immediately from within your own agency, or you may need to take the client yourself to his own general practitioner, or to your local accident and emergency unit for an assessment by a psychiatric doctor. Occasionally your client may live with reliable and willing relatives who understand the responsibilities and are able to fulfil them. A safe environment is vital. As a counsellor your responsibility is to assess. Clients with an immediate, lethal and precise suicide plan will require a safe environment or hospitalisation. You may need to go outside the realms of the confidential relationship to prevent ideation becoming reality (see Chapters 1 and 4).

The Role of Questionnaires

There are many questionnaires available which will help you assess the suicidal potential of the individual. The advantages of such forms are that they can enhance the effectiveness of the assessment (Bloom and Fischer, 1982). These questionnaires enable you to make a rapid and efficient assessment, and are generally easy to administer. The forms are readily available and provide access to information about the client which may be hard to observe overtly. By using questionnaires you can make comparisons with some established norms or compare your client's progress with their previous score. You need to bear in mind that any score is simply an estimate and should not be accepted uncritically. It is better to use the questionnaires and their scores as an assessment instrument to monitor progress. They are most helpful when used in conjunction with other methods of evaluating progress.

Some useful questionnaires in detecting suicide are:

1 reasons for living scale (Linehan, 1985) to measure adaptive characteristics in suicide
2 scale for suicide ideation (Beck et al., 1971)
3 hopelessness scale (Beck et al., 1974b) to assess degree of suicide risk
4 prediction of suicide scale (Beck et al., 1974a)
5 Los Angeles suicide prevention scale (Los Angeles Center for Suicide Prevention, 1973)
6 Beck depression inventory (Beck, 1978).

Summary: the Key Points for Weighing the Risk of Suicide

■ *Age and sex* The potential is greater for men than women and for persons over 65.
■ *Symptoms* The potential is greater if the individual is depressed, cannot sleep, feels hopeless, or is a known substance abuser.

- *Stress* The potential is greater if the individual is under tremendous stress.
- *Suicidal plan* The potential is greater with increases in the lethality, structure, and detail of the plan.
- *Support* The potential is greater if the individual has no family or friends.
- *Prior suicide attempts* The potential is greater if the individual has a past history of suicidal attempts.
- *Interpersonal aspects* The potential is greater if the individual has no outlet or has been rejected by others.
- *Physical illness* The potential is greater if there is debilitating or chronic illness.

Practice Points

Any person who wishes to end their life may find a way to do so.

Remain aware of the factors which have been identified for those most at risk of suicide.

People who have a psychiatric disorder have a (statistically) high incidence of suicide.

The majority of people who commit suicide have made their intentions known to at least one other person.

Take all messages about suicide seriously. Do not be afraid to explore suicidal ideation with your client. This does not make suicidal behaviour more likely.

A previous attempt of suicide is an important predictor that suicide may be contemplated in the future.

Clients with an immediate, lethal and precise suicide plan will require a safe environment or hospitalisation.

Questionnaires are helpful in assessing the suicide potential of individuals and most helpful when used in conjunction with other assessment methods.

Medical Condition

Medical illness is often accompanied by unrecognised psychiatric morbidity which, unless treated, may lead to psychiatric disorder and suicide (Saunders and Valente, 1988). In primary care, high suicide rates occur among clients with cancer, AIDS, chronic illness, substance abuse and depression.

In a study by Eastwood and Trevelyan (1972) involving a randomly chosen sample of the general population, it was found that there was a positive association between physical and psychiatric disorder. In general practice, it has been consistently found in surveys that clients with psychiatric illness have a very high incidence of physical morbidity (Shepherd et al., 1966). The incidence of physical disorder increases with age.

In medical hospital wards, surveys have shown that over a quarter of inpatients have psychiatric disorders (Querido, 1959). Following his research, Querido suggested that psychiatric disorder may interfere with recovery from physical illness.

Interplay of Psychological Factors on Physical Illness
As early as Tuke (1872) it was discovered that psychological factors played an important role in the aetiology of physical illness. From these beginnings emerged the theory of psychosomatic medicine (Bynum, 1983). More modern theories accept that physical illness has multiple causes (Engel, 1962). Research has also focused on the role of stressful life events in precipitating physical illness (Holmes and Rahe, 1967).

Some physical conditions, treatments and drugs may cause symptoms resembling psychiatric disorders. Clients are more vulnerable, if they have experienced a psychiatric disorder in the past, to further psychiatric disorder when developing a severe physical illness (Campbell, 1986). Certain kinds of physical illness are more likely to provoke serious psychiatric consequences. These include illnesses requiring long unpleasant treatments such as radiotherapy, life-threatening illnesses, illnesses with prolonged suffering and pain, and treatments which require surgical removal. Some psychological symptoms may be directly triggered by physical illness (Table 3.6).

There are some commonly used drugs which can also produce psychiatric symptoms: see the non-exhaustive list in Table 3.7. Whenever, during your information gathering, you discover your client is taking medication, consider the possibility that their symptoms may have been induced by their particular medication. For more detailed information see Davies (1987).

You may ask, 'Why is all this information necessary'? When assessing health factors, you are also assessing suitability for

Table 3.6 *Physical illness and psychological symptoms*

Physical illness	Psychological symptoms
Cancer, infections, dementias, diabetes, thyroid disorder, Addison's disease	Depression
Neurological disorders, hypoglycaemia, hyperventilation, drug withdrawal, hyperthyroidism	Anxiety
Cancer, Cushing's syndrome, Addison's disease, diabetes, anaemia, radiotherapy, chronic infection	Fatigue
Peripheral neuropathy, arthritis, pain, muscle disorder	Weakness
Cancer, diabetes, tuberculosis, hyperthyroidism	Loss of weight

Table 3.7 *Drugs creating psychiatric symptoms*

Drugs	Symptoms
Analgesic, e.g., opiates (morphine, codeine)	Mood disorder
Anti-inflammatory e.g., Indocid, Brufen, baclofen	Depression
Anticonvulsants, e.g., phenytoin, primidone, carbamazepine	
Antihistamines, e.g., Triludan, Dimotane	
Antihypertensive agents, e.g., methyldopa, clonidine	
Oral contraceptives	
Neuroleptics, e.g., haloperidol, fluphenazine	
Anti-microbials, e.g., Cycloserine, norfloxacin	
Anti-parkinsonian agents, e.g., Levadopa	
Central nervous system depressants, e.g., hypnotics, sedatives, alcohol	Delirium
Anticonvulsants	
Antihistamines	
Anticholinergic drugs, e.g., betablockers, digoxin	
Hallucinogenic drugs	Psychiatric
Betablockers	symptoms
Corticosteroids	
Appetite suppressants	
Neuroleptics, e.g., haloperidol	Behaviour
Benzodiazepines, e.g., diazepam, corazepam	disturbance

treatment. Your client may not tell you that she has a physical health problem, and this may be for a number of reasons. It is possible that your client does not realise the connection between mind and body. She may be ashamed and find it hard to talk about having contracted HIV, or may have a drug or alcohol

Table 3.8 *Typical questions to ask your client*

Question	Reason for asking
Has she seen a doctor?	Exploration of feelings, such as fear of doctors or hospitals. Mistrust of medical profession
How long has she experienced the problem? How often does it occur? When is it worse?	Indication of interference in everyday life
Are any medications being currently taken?	May affect client's mood, physiology or behaviour
What is the dosage and how often is it taken?	Effects may be very different dependent on body weight and age
Who prescribed the medication?	Indication of awareness of physical condition, or use of over-the-counter medication. Is client already seeing a psychiatrist, is medication being monitored regularly?
Family's past medical history: who died when and of what? Was it lingering or agonising?	Ascertain feelings regarding health and illness. Death of someone close may have marked effect on client

problem. Whatever the reasons, you are advised not to avoid talking about her health. It is possible that your client will feel uncomfortable or experience fear when this issue is raised. Be sensitive. Encourage further exploration of what the physical symptoms might mean to her. It is important to know how your client sees these symptoms in relation to her presenting problem. If your client has spoken about concerns regarding her health, it provides you with the opportunity to further discuss her health, but remember it is your job to obtain factual information and not to diagnose a medical condition. When your client has been forthcoming about a physical symptom or illness, this opens up other areas for assessment. See Table 3.8 for examples of typical assessment questions to ask your client.

The environment in which you work will to some extent determine when and what you will ask about your client's health. If you work in a hospital or outpatients department you may well have a full medical history prior to meeting your client. If you work in a GP surgery you may have access to your client's medical notes. Wherever you work, I advise that you write down this information and think carefully about how your client may respond to their recognition of these health problems: each client may have different thoughts, feelings and meanings about health and illness. All this information is likely to enable you to be more helpful to your client and offer the most suitable therapy.

Practice Points

Psychological factors play an important role in the aetiology of physical illness.

Some physical conditions, treatment and drugs may cause symptoms resembling psychiatric disorder.

Be sensitive when enquiring about your client's physical health.

Remember there are a number of commonly used drugs which can also produce psychiatric symptoms. This is why it is helpful to ask your client if she or he is taking medication.

There is a clear connection between physical health and psychological health.

Conclusion

In this chapter I have considered a wide range of material about medical and psychiatric assessment. Much detailed information has been provided, some of which trainee counsellors, as well as experienced therapists who do not have a working knowledge of psychiatry, may find difficult to assimilate initially. Chapter 1 has outlined some of the broader issues concerning diagnosis, and it is hoped that you will allow yourself to gradually absorb these important aspects of assessment into your practice rather than becoming overwhelmed with the mass of information presented. Some sections of the counselling fraternity have tended to ignore psychiatric and medical aspects of assessment, sometimes to the detriment of the client. I hope that this chapter has introduced some of the important concerns which might otherwise go undetected.

References

American Psychiatric Association (1994) *Diagnostic and Statistical Manual of Mental Disorders* (4th edn). Washington, DC: APA.

Appleby, L. and Forshaw, D. (1990) *Post Graduate Psychiatry Clinical Foundations*. Oxford: Heinemann Medical Books.

Beck, A.T. (1978) *Depression Inventory*. Philadelphia: Center for Cognitive Therapy.

Beck, A.T., Kovacs, M. and Weissman, A. (1971) 'Assessment of suicidal ideation: the scale for suicidal ideation', *Journal of Consultancy and Clinical Psychology*, 47: 343–52.

Beck, A.T., Schuyler, D. and Herman, I. (1974a) 'Development of suicidal intent scales', in A.T. Beck, H.L.P. Resnick and D.J. Lettie (eds), *The Prediction of Suicide*. Maryland: Charles Press.

Beck, A.T., Weissman, A., Lester, D. and Trexter, L. (1974b) 'The measurement of pessimism: the hopelessness scale', *Journal of Consulting and Clinical Psychology*, 42: 861–5.

Bloom, M. and Fischer, J. (1982) *Evaluating Practice: Guidelines for the Accountable Professional*. Englewood Cliffs, NJ: Prentice-Hall.

Bynum, W.F. (1983) 'Psychiatry in its historical context', in M. Shepherd and O.L. Zangwill (eds), *Handbook of Psychiatry*, vol. 1. Cambridge: Cambridge University Press.

Campbell, T.L. (1986) *Families' Impact on Health: a World Review and Annotated Bibliography*. NIMH Series DN6. Washington, DC: US Government Policy Office.

Davies, D.M. (1987) *Textbook of Adverse Drug Reactions* (3rd edn). Oxford: Oxford University Press.

Eastwood, R. and Trevelyan, M.H. (1972) 'Relationship between physical and psychiatric disorder', *Psychological Medicine*, 2: 363–72.

Engel, G. (1962) *Psychological Development in Health and Disease*. Philadelphia: Saunders.

Freud, S. (1911) 'Psychoanalytic notes upon an autobiographical account of cases of paranoia (Schreber)', in *The Complete Psychological Works* (standard edn), vol. 12. London: Hogarth Press, 1958. pp. 1–82.

Heikkinen, M., Aro, H. and Lonnquist, J. (1994) 'Recent life events, social support and suicide', *Acta Psychiatr. Scand.*, suppl. 377: 65–72.

Holmes, T. and Rahe, R.H. (1967) 'The social adjustment rating scale', *Journal of Psychosomatic Research*, 11, 213–18.

Institute of Psychiatry (1973) *Notes on Eliciting and Recording Clinical Information*. Oxford: Oxford University Press.

Kingdom, D.G. and Turkington, D. (1994) *Cognitive-Behavioural Therapy of Schizophrenia*. Hove: Lawrence Erlbaum, Ltd.

Leff, J.P. and Isaacs, A.D. (1990) *Psychiatric Examination in Clinical Practice*. Oxford: Blackwell.

Linehan, Marsha M. (1985) 'The reason for living scale', in P.A. Keller and L.G. Ritts (eds), *Innovations in Clinical Practice: a Source Book*, vol. 4. Sarasota, FL: Professional Resource Exchange.

Los Angeles Center for Suicide Prevention (1973) *Los Angeles Suicide Prevention Scale*. Los Angeles: LACSP.

Lukas, S. (1993) *Where to Start and What to Ask: an Assessment Handbook*. London: W.W. Norton.

Marzuk, P., Tierney, H., Tardiff, K., Gross, E., Morgan, E., Hsu, M.A. and Mann, J. (1988) 'Increased risk of suicide in persons with AIDS', *Journal of the American Medical Association*, 259(9): 1333–7.

Morrison, J. (1995) *The First Interview*. New York: Guilford Press.

Post, F. (1965) *The Clinical Psychiatry of Late Life*. New York: Pergamon Press.

Querido, A. (1959) 'Forecast and follow-up: an investigation into the clinical, social and mental factors determining the results of hospital treatment', *British Journal of Preventive and Social Medicine*, 13: 334–9.

Rack, P. (1982) *Race, Culture and Mental Disorder*. London: Routledge. pp. 121–2.

Retterstol, N. (1993) *Suicide: a European Perspective*. Cambridge: Cambridge University Press.

Robins, E., Gassner, S., Kayes, J., Wilkinson, R.H. and Murphy, G.E. (1959) 'The communication of suicidal intent: a study of 134 successful (completed) suicides', *American Journal of Psychiatry*, 115: 724–33.

Rose, N.D.B. (ed.) (1994) *Essential Psychiatry* (2nd edn). Oxford: Blackwell Scientific.

Roy, A. (1982) 'Risk factors for suicide in psychiatric patients', *Archives of General Psychiatry*, 39: 1089–95.

Roy, A. (1992) 'Marked reductions in indexes of dopamine metabolism among patients with depression who attempted suicide', *Archives of General Psychiatry*, 49: 447–50.

Saunders, J.M. and Valente, S.M. (1988) 'Cancer and suicide', *Oncology Nursing Forum*, 15(5): 575–80.

Schneider, K. (1949) 'The concept of delusion', reprinted and translated in S.R. Hirsch and M. Shepherd (eds), *Themes and Variations in European Psychiatry*. Bristol: John Wright, 1974.

Shaffer, D. (1974) 'Suicide in childhood and early adolescence', *Journal of Child Psychology and Psychiatry*, 15: 275–91.

Shepherd, M., Cooper, B., Brown, A.C. and Kalton, G.W. (1966) *Psychiatric Illness in General Practice*. London: Oxford University Press.

Stengel, E. (1952) 'Enquiries into attempted suicide', *Proceedings of the Royal Society of Medicine*, 45: 613–20.

Stengel, E. and Cook, N.G. (1958) *Attempted Suicide: its Social Significance and Effects*. Maudsley Monograph no. 4. London: Chapman and Hall.

Symonds, R.L. (1985) 'Psychiatric aspects of railway fatalities', *Psychological Medicine*, 15: 609–21.

Tuke, D.H. (1872) *Illustrations of the Influence of the Mind upon the Body in Health and Disease*. London: J. and A. Churchill.

Wechsler, D. (1945) 'A standardised memory scale for clinical use', *Journal of Psychology*, 19: 87–95.

Wing, J.K., Cooper, J.E. and Sartorius, N. (1974) *Measurement and Classification of Psychiatric Symptoms*. Cambridge: Cambridge University Press.

World Health Organisation (1992) *International Classifications of Diseases* (10th edn). Geneva: WHO.

4 *What Type of Help?*

Peter Ruddell and Berni Curwen

Readiness and Suitability of Client for Counselling

Client's Recognition of Difficulties and Insight into Them

A client who seeks counselling is likely to have already acknowledged that they have a problem or that they would like to change some aspects of their life. This acknowledgement is necessary in order that they are able to engage in therapy. It may be thought of as a spectrum from slight to profound understanding. Where such insight is minimal, a person may have been encouraged to seek counselling by another person, such as a partner, family members, employers etc., but believes the 'problem' to be largely outside of herself. Otherwise, the person will probably have engaged in a process of reflection into her situation, to at least some extent. It is possible that the person has not spoken about her problem to another individual at all, or in any great depth, and her ideas about the situation may be relatively undeveloped. Similarly, the person's understanding about her problem may be oblique and focused on the least important aspects, as the case example in Chapter 5 about alcohol misuse demonstrates.

Readiness for counselling also requires that individuals recognise, if only in a small way, that they contribute to their difficulties. At the start of therapy, this insight into the problem is likely to be superficial, intellectual, or in some cases non-existent; it is only by working through various issues and problems over the course of therapy that the client will deepen this understanding to achieve emotional insight (Ellis, 1963).

A person may appear to be ready for counselling, in recognising the problem as discussed above, but be unwilling to invest time and effort in the process. Yet, in part, the counsellor's task may be to encourage the client's motivation (Miller and Rollnick, 1991) and understanding through helping them to recognise the links between their thoughts, feelings and actions and their current problems.

The individual may be willing to work on their problem, yet in some way be unable to work in a particular therapeutic framework. For example, a person who is totally unable to recognise the interaction of thoughts, feelings and actions will be unlikely to benefit from the cognitive-behavioural therapies if preliminary attempts to orientate the client into the particular framework are unsuccessful. Similarly, a person who is quite unable to recognise the significance of earlier intrapsychic conflict for their current problems, even after the therapist has assisted with this understanding (through interpretations), is unlikely to benefit from psychodynamic therapy.

When a potential client has engaged in counselling or other forms of help (such as self-help, group work etc.) this may have been experienced as in some way helpful or unhelpful. This will have significance now; for example, if the person found a particular approach to be helpful in the past, a similar approach might be suitable again. Yet, this is worth checking out further, as it could also suggest compliance, or ignorance of other therapeutic approaches which might be more suitable now. Where a person has found the experience of previous counselling to be unhelpful, it is fruitful to explore the reasons, to help prevent this from happening again. This is discussed in greater depth in Dryden and Feltham (1994). Previous counselling may have been experienced as unhelpful for a number of reasons. The therapist may have been ineffective with this client. The type of therapy offered may not have suited the individual's style. The rationale for therapy may not have been (adequately) explained in approaches where this is crucial (such as behaviour therapy). The match between client and therapist may have been unsuitable (for example, gender or culture). There may be many other reasons too and it is important to check these out to minimise the risk of duplicating past failures. But not all unhelpful experiences are necessarily the fault of the therapist, or indeed, avoidable.

The Person's Position in Psychosocial Development

Chapter 5 looks in some detail at the concept of psychosocial development as viewed through Erikson's eight-stage model and the possible need to work through blocks to development at a later stage in life. The most appropriate type of help for a person may be partly determined by his or her position in the developmental structure. For example, a person might experience lack of assertiveness as only a minor difficulty as a teenager, but as a major problem later on in life in a stressful working environment. Similarly, an adolescent attempting to form intimate relationships may need to experience some turmoil in facing life in order to develop as an individual and not necessarily require formal help at this stage.

The Individual's Motivation to Engage in Personal Work

We noted earlier that motivation to engage in personal work is unlikely if the person has no recognition of his or her part in the problem, although there may be other exceptions: counselling as part of a court order may be seen as preferable to prison! Similarly, a person may be very strongly encouraged by their employer to engage in counselling.

Motivation in such non-consensual counselling might initially be lacking, yet the counsellor may in some cases be able to develop this by helping the client to appreciate some benefits of the process. Likewise, a person with a somatic problem, such as one in which there are observable and identifiable disturbances of bodily functioning, might nevertheless come to recognise that they can achieve at least some control through psychological means, if skilfully aided by the therapist.

Some people who apparently desire counselling, and to this extent are motivated to seek help, nevertheless expect change to come from outside of themselves. This expectation may be approached in a variety of ways by different therapies and these people need not necessarily be denied counselling if they can be helped to recognise their input into their own problems. This input may be causative or perpetuating, but with help may become curative. Such counsellor-aided insight will be very useful when an individual isolates herself from her central problem to the extent that she does not recognise that she has a problem. Tom, in Chapter 5, who apparently failed to recognise the extent of his drinking problem, is a good example.

Some individuals who recognise their part in the problem may strongly desire a rapid solution and consequently be poorly motivated towards therapies which are of longer duration and not overtly pertinent to their immediate concerns. Here, personality factors may interact with therapeutic approaches and these require different types of personal work which a particular individual may be more or less inclined to engage in. For example, cognitive-behavioural therapy may require a person to complete a 'daily log' of their problems and the person may be unwilling to do this. Such reluctance would need to be explored, as it may be part of the problem for which they seek help. This may be connected with the person's belief that there is or is not the possibility for personal change and that a given approach may or may not be helpful in achieving it. Certain therapies rely more heavily than others on providing the client with a clear rationale for the particular process of therapy and consider this essential for a client to be able to give informed consent to therapy. The cognitive-behavioural therapies provide a clear rationale whereas the psychodynamic therapies generally do not (and their clients may not benefit from such an explanation).

Fluctuations in motivation are common during therapy and can often be helpful in guiding the therapist towards and through the client's blocks and difficulties.

Practical Aspects of Client Commitment

There are a number of practical aspects which may have a bearing on the client's degree of commitment. These can be discussed prior to counselling. First is the cost. If you or your agency charges the client directly (as opposed to indirect charging such as through the NHS) the set fee or the details of a sliding scale of costs will hopefully have been divulged to the client prior to your meeting, and now is a good time to ensure that the details have been correctly understood.

Secondly, time. The counsellor should advise the client about the probable time commitment involved if therapy is offered as an option:

1   How long will each session last?
2   How frequent will the sessions be?
3   When will the sessions be? It is often helpful to have a regular day and time for sessions to enable the client to plan ahead,

but counsellor flexibility is important, such as when a person's work involves shifts!

4 What will be the duration of therapy? It may not be possible to define exactly the length of time over which therapy will extend. An initial series of sessions can be negotiated, after which the effectiveness of the approach can be evaluated and further sessions agreed if necessary.

A third consideration is travel and is linked with the time element which we have just discussed. It may be that a client has been referred or recommended to you or your agency and that she lives some distance away. If this is so, it will be helpful to discuss the practical implications with her before she becomes involved with your agency so that a rational decision can be made. If the potential client lives a considerable distance from you, there may be a suitable therapist who is located more locally to her. Where your agency specialises in a particular field which pertains to your client's problems or concerns he or she may be willing to travel the distance involved. The decision you come to with the individual may be influenced, in part, by the (probable) duration and frequency of therapy. Extended sessions, for example of two hours, may be suitable in some cases where a client has to travel some distance. The cost of travel may also be a consideration. Telephone counselling may be appropriate in some situations (Rosenfield, 1996). Particularly where public transport is involved, your agency's policy on late arrivals or missed appointments may be helpfully discussed at this point.

Temporary Factors Affecting Client's Suitability for Counselling

Where there appear to be temporary factors affecting the potential client's suitability for counselling, it is usually good practice to discuss these with the person. There may be occasions where the individual is temporarily unsuitable for your particular agency, for example, where a person is severely depressed and requires inpatient care which your agency does not offer.

We have already discussed above how the person's experience of previous counselling may (temporarily) affect her current suitability. Your agency's scale of fees may be unsuitable for the client at the present time! A person who is already in counselling

Table 4.1 *Illnesses with associated psychological symptoms*

Illness	Psychological symptoms
Neurosyphilis	Depression, psychosis, confusion
Myxoedema	Depression
Thyrotoxicosis	Anxiety, psychosis
Anaemia	Depression
Cushing's syndrome	Depression
Subdural haematoma	Confusion, depression
Vitamin deficiency	Apathy, mood instability, delusions, hallucinations (rare)
Phaeochromocytoma	Anxiety, confusion (rare)
Acute porphyria	Psychosis, depression
Hyperparathyroidism	Depression, inertia, irritability
Hypoparathyroidism	Depression nervousness
Hypopituitarism	Depression, apathy, somnolence

may sometimes experience a major life event which temporarily interrupts the course of therapy, or in some cases brings it to an abrupt end altogether. For example, a person might unexpectedly and unavoidably be required to travel abroad during the course of her work for a limited period of time. Occasionally, a severe and disabling illness might bring therapy to a permanent halt, although its permanency might be reassessed over the course of time.

Illnesses sometimes have associated psychological aspects which may spontaneously remit when the illness has run its course or is successfully treated. Counselling interventions would not normally be appropriate in such situations, except when supportive therapy is thought to be helpful. A non-exhaustive list is given in Table 4.1. Conversely, some illnesses such as heart disease, diabetes or cancer might have profound consequences for a person who may benefit from counselling interventions.

Some drugs, both prescribed and illicit, may lead to psychological disturbances which will remit when the drug is discontinued; in some cases, the disturbances may continue. Chapter 3 on medical and psychiatric assessment considers this further. Often, conveying this information to the person may be all that is necessary. Where illicit drugs and/or long-term use (such as Ativan, alcohol) are involved, counselling is often required and specialist agencies are often most helpful, particularly where help in withdrawing from the addiction is needed.

Psychiatric disorders are considered in Chapter 3, where it is seen that a wide range of interventions are usually considered appropriate for different conditions. (See also Chapter 1.) Where counselling is not thought to be the preferred primary intervention for a given condition or person, it may nevertheless be indicated in parallel with other therapy at certain points in a person's life. For example, a person receiving drug therapy for schizophrenia might also require interpersonal interventions to assist them in coping with the consequences of the illness (see, for example, Falloon et al., 1984), or to help them in overcoming problems for which other people commonly seek help. In psychiatric illnesses with a psychotic component, it is acknowledged that a psychotic episode can be triggered by stressful events: see for example Brown and Birley (1968). Overly confrontative forms of therapy might therefore be contra-indicated with this client group. While there had emerged a general consensus that people who are actively psychotic should not be engaged in counselling, a number of practitioners have pioneered work which challenges this view (see Kingdom and Turkington, 1991).

Practice Points

Keep the following in mind as you assess a potential client's suitability for counselling. To what extent does she:

- acknowledge the problem?
- recognise her own contribution to the difficulties?
- demonstrate motivation?

Discuss any previous counselling the client may have had and use the response to help you decide whether particular therapeutic frameworks are especially indicated or not.

Be aware of the client's position in psychosocial development.

Discuss cost, time, place, regularity and possible duration of therapy with client. Consider telephone counselling if necessary.

Temporary factors may affect the client's suitability for counselling: discuss these with her.

Counselling may not be the primary or sole form of intervention: consider it in parallel with other interventions.

What Type of Counselling?

A number of dimensions can be considered in deciding upon the type of counselling likely to be of most benefit to an individual with the concerns they present. We shall present four areas for consideration:

1 duration of therapy
2 number in therapy
3 whether or not to use an agency specialising in a particular problem
4 type of therapeutic orientation (this is discussed in Chapters 1 and 5 and will not be considered further here).

Duration of Therapy

Therapy might take place over a short or long period, and is perhaps best considered as a continuum with brief therapy at one end and long-term therapy at the other. Different counsellors and organisations have varying views as to what constitutes 'brief therapy'; these intermesh with the type of therapeutic orientation. For example, Malan (1979) has used 30 sessions as a cut-off for brief psychodynamic therapy whereas Dryden (1995) has more recently outlined an 11 session protocol for brief rational emotive behaviour therapy. These alternative timescales are partly a reflection of the different work involved dependent upon the therapeutic orientation from which it is derived.

Both of the above practitioners have developed protocols to guide them in determining whether or not a person (with their current problems) is suitable for planned brief therapy. The reader is referred to the references above for a detailed outline of these protocols, but the following criteria seem to represent the core elements of both:

1 The person's problems are capable of clear identification, allowing a precise focus for therapy to be determined, and appear to be able to be sufficiently resolved within the brief timespan.
2 The person has responded positively to the type of therapeutic work being offered either at first contact or during the initial session.

3 The person has sufficient understanding and motivation to work within the framework offered.
4 There are no major contra-indications.

Having outlined the above criteria, it is important to note that there is no complete consensus within the counselling fraternity about who is suitable for 'brief therapy'. Again, a continuum of practitioners can be imagined, with those advocating strict criteria for inclusion in brief therapy at one end (Davanloo, 1978) and those who are less stringent at the other end (Budman and Gurman, 1988; Ellis, 1996).

Some of the most commonly encountered problem areas which often benefit from brief therapy are as follows:

- simple phobias
- assertiveness
- anxiety management
- stress management
- depression (dependent on severity)
- sexual difficulties.

The criteria for brief therapy outlined above do not preclude work on long-standing (that is, chronic) problems; it is possible to work with a person in brief therapy who has long-standing psychological problems (which are not incapacitating) but who wishes to work on an identified and focused problem. Brief therapy has even been used to help individuals with narcissistic and borderline personality disorder (Lazarus, 1982; Liebovitch, 1983; Winston et al., 1991). A formal assessment of an individual's psychological functioning is advocated by Malan (1980) and discussed in Chapter 3. This will also provide suitable material from which any contra-indications for brief therapy may be identified.

A form of intervention which is brief, and is usually considered the particular domain of community psychiatry, is crisis intervention. Crisis intervention has developed from the work of Lindemann (1944) and Caplan (1961). For people who are well motivated and have stable personalities, a crisis (that is, a major but transitory difficulty) can be used as an opportunity to discover new ways of coping where the person's previous coping strategies have failed. A multidisciplinary team is usually involved in this type of work. Some difficulties which have responded well to this approach include disturbed behaviour or emotions in response to social crisis (for example self-harm or substance abuse following a relationship breakdown), severe life disruptions and natural disasters.

In discussing planned brief therapy, above, it was noted that some counsellors have more stringent criteria for inclusion; this is not to suggest that all other therapy need be long! The counsellor seeks to provide the minimum intervention consistent with the changes thought appropriate by client and counsellor. Parry (1992), in considering the work of Howard et al. (1986), has noted that 'most therapy, even as practised in long-term settings, remains short-term due to attrition, hence planned short-term therapies may actually result in longer exposure to treatments'.

Nevertheless, some people or problem areas may require longer-term work. For example, people with severe and long-lasting mental health problems such as schizophrenia, manic depression and obsessive compulsive disorder, and people presenting with personality disorders, may require relatively long-term help, including supportive therapy. For a clear outline of supportive therapy, see Bloch (1986). A supportive relationship can easily develop into a dependent relationship, particularly where one individual provides most of the support. For this reason, support is often best provided by a number of individuals, such as a self-help group (see below) or some other supportive environment, such as a day centre.

How Many in Therapy?
Therapy can take place with a varying number of individuals, from one person engaged in self-help, to a large group of people such as a personal growth group. The therapist will often take the lead in deciding whether individual, couple, group or other therapy is most suitable for a particular person or problem. 'Many problems, both in individuals and in relationships, can be helped in several different ways, and ultimately in many cases the choice of therapeutic approach is arbitrary' (Crowe and Ridley, 1990). With growing public awareness of counselling, it is probable that people will take a more prominent role in the decision-making process.

All problems for which counselling is suitable have been tackled through individual therapy and some therapists offer only this paradigm. Individual therapy has the obvious benefit that more time and attention can be given to the individual seeking help. This might be particularly necessary where detailed behavioural work is called for. There are many types of problem for which individual and group work are equally suitable and effective. In such cases cost may be a consideration. The view of the client should be considered, although in some instances this may be clouded by the problem for which they are seeking help. For example a person who requires help with relationship difficulties may seek individual help to avoid further friction with their partner, although work with the couple would be preferable. Where a person's judgement seems to be clouded in this way, it is helpful to discuss this openly with the potential client. In some circumstances, where the therapist has good reason to believe that group therapy would be especially appropriate, it may be beneficial to offer the client a few initial sessions of individual therapy followed by group therapy. For example, a person experiencing social anxiety might benefit from such an approach.

Couple therapy is often the preferred option when the relationship between a couple is the main problem, or where an individual's problem has major repercussions upon the relationship and is amenable to couple therapy, such as a phobia of sex existing prior to the beginning of the relationship (Jacobson and Gurman, 1995). Couple therapy may also be combined in some circumstances with individual therapy or with family therapy; Crowe and Ridley (1990) consider some of the factors which are important in deciding whether or not couple therapy is appropriate, as follows:

1 The problem seems to be connected with the relationship.
2 The couple are willing to attend together (even when there is initial reluctance of one partner).
3 The relationship is continuing.
4 The individual's problem is not too acute for couple therapy at present.

Some of the most appropriate problems for couple therapy are when arguments and marital tension are causing concern, when one partner experiences increased stress following the improvement of the other as a result of individual therapy (Crowe and

Ridley, 1990), or when one partner spends much of an individual session complaining about the other partner's behaviour (Ackerman, 1966).

Couple therapy has also proved effective in many cases of alcohol abuse (O'Farrell, 1994) and domestic violence (Wile, 1993), where therapy 'examines violence within the context of the [marital] relationship rather than concentrating on one individual as the source of violence' provided that 'there is no immediate threat of further violence' (Shapiro, 1988).

Family therapy involves one or more family members, and although the work often centres around the nuclear family, it may also involve the extended family. While family therapy has prominently used systems theory (Minuchin, 1974; Schwarz, 1994), any other theoretical orientation may be involved. Although systems theory may not necessarily be subscribed to by the therapist(s), the focus is primarily upon family relationships rather than the individual. While therapy may focus on a particular grouping of family members, such as mother, father and their two daughters, some sessions will not always involve all members of this group.

The major factors which are usually necessary for effective family therapy to be used are as follows:

1 The problem seems to be connected with family relationships.
2 The family unit is willing to attend together (even when there is initial reluctance of one or more members).
3 The family relationship is continuing.
4 The problems of individual family members are not too acute for family therapy at present, such as a person who is currently experiencing acute paranoid psychosis.
5 Attendance is not precluded on the grounds of geographical location or time constraints (for example where members work opposite shifts).

Family therapy has been successfully used to treat problems that have not responded to other treatment approaches, and has been helpful with the following:

- alcohol misuse (Shapiro, 1982; Kaufman and Kaufman, 1981)
- domestic violence (Shapiro, 1986)
- eating disorders (Minuchin et al., 1978)

- emotional disorders in children and adolescents (Shapiro, 1980)
- schizophrenia (Falloon et al., 1984)
- substance abuse (Kaufman and Kaufman, 1981).

In discussing couple therapy, above, it was noted that while there may sometimes be indicators to strongly suggest couple therapy in certain situations, there are many circumstances in which other modes of therapy might be equally effective. The same can be said of family therapy and group therapy too: this is particularly true of group therapy, where the problems addressed are also commonly approached through individual therapy. Similarly, group therapy may proceed through any one of a variety of therapeutic approaches, such as existential, behavioural, Gestalt, transactional analysis, etc. and a variety of group sizes.

The therapeutic approach, the make-up of the group in terms of its members, and the style and characteristics of the therapist will all influence the experience an individual derives from a group. What groups have in common is 'the context of a group and the hope of the members that they will derive some special benefit from their membership *for problems that have been framed, by and large, in interpersonal terms*' (Bloch, 1988: 288). Bloch has identified a number of therapeutic factors that operate across a range of different therapeutic orientations:

- *Self-disclosure*: revealing personal information to the group.
- *Self-understanding (insight)*: learning something important about oneself.
- *Acceptance (cohesiveness)*: sense of belonging and being valued.
- *Learning from interpersonal action*: the attempt to relate constructively and adaptively within the group.
- *Catharsis*: ventilation of feelings, which brings relief.
- *Guidance*: receiving information or advice.
- *Universality*: the sense that one is not unique in one's problems.
- *Altruism*: the sense that one can be of value to others.
- *Vicarious learning*: learning about oneself through the observation of other group members, including the therapist.
- *Instillation of hope*: gaining a sense of optimism about the potential for progress.

Groups usually contain individuals who may each experience different types of problem, and some people attend groups in order to help bring about 'personal growth'. However, there are also groups which focus on specific problems, and a small sample of these is given below:

- agoraphobia
- anger management
- anxiety management
- confidence building
- eating disorders
- flying phobia
- interpersonal relationship difficulties
- sexual abuse (once the individual is suitably prepared)
- social anxiety
- social phobia
- stress management.

Groups set up for specific problem areas, such as those above, may be led by a trained therapist, but groups also exist which may not have a facilitator and these are discussed in the section below about self-help. Some such focal problems have agencies devoted to helping people who are affected by them.

Specific Problem Agencies

A number of organisations have developed, both nationally and locally, offering counselling to people suffering from specific types of problem. These vary considerably in the type of service offered. They range from agencies which may only provide counselling, such as a local organisation set up to provide counselling to adult female survivors of sexual abuse, to those providing a range of services and support – including counselling – such as some drug and alcohol misuse services, which may offer advice, detoxification and support in addition to individual counselling.

Such agencies also range widely in the delivery of the counselling service, from those which employ accredited counsellors to those which largely use voluntary trainee counsellors under supervision; this extends to those led by users, which will be considered further when we discuss self-help. Organisations also differ in the cost of their services to the individual, which may be an important factor in their selection. These variations interact with whether or not the organisation is charitable, private, public or statutory. In some cases, several organisations join together to offer a service.

Examples of some of the problems around which agencies have offered specific help are as follows:

- AIDS and HIV
- alcohol misuse
- bereavement
- cancer
- disfigurement
- eating disorders
- relationship problems (such as Relate)
- sexual abuse
- sexual problems
- substance misuse.

Given the wide variation of services and their delivery noted above, it is not surprising that they may vary considerably in their effectiveness. They may have a number of positive features in common. First, the counsellors specialising in a particular field may develop an advanced knowledge and information base for their specialism. Secondly, the counsellors may develop greater empathy from understanding all aspects of a problem and the impact they may have on an individual's life. Thirdly, for some such problem areas, this may enable an organisation to develop a particular culture which helps the user to feel better understood and accepted. Fourthly, they may have a destigmatising effect, in bringing the problem into public prominence and in accepting the people who have the problem. Fifthly, they may be involved in research which will be of benefit to future sufferers.

In considering 'what type of counselling' we have largely assumed that counselling is distinct from other types of help. However, the line which divides counselling from other forms of help may in some instances be somewhat tenuous; 'self-help' groups and certain helplines are such examples. In the next section, we will consider forms of help other than counselling which a practitioner may benefit from being aware of when assessing a person.

Practice Points

Consider using brief therapy where

- the client's problem can clearly be identified
- the client has responded positively to the particular approach being considered (for example cognitive-behavioural therapy or psycho-dynamic therapy)
- the client has sufficient understanding and motivation to work using the framework
- there are no contra-indications.

Limit therapy to the shortest time possible, commensurate with appropriate intervention.

Where counselling is appropriate, discuss with your client whether this would best be:

- one to one
- couple counselling
- family therapy
- group therapy.

Remember that where a preferred option is not available, other approaches may be considered.

Remember that a wide range of agencies exist to help people with specific problems: these may or may not be available in your locality.

Other Types of Help

We have already discussed therapeutic groups, led by a counsellor, in the section above. In assessing an individual, it is sometimes apparent that he would benefit from a group in addition to, or instead of, individual therapeutic work. This may be achieved by encouraging the person to attend a self-help peer group, or a support group. Owing to geographical location, absolute choice may not always be possible.

Self-help and support groups are not distinct categories. However, self-help groups tend to be for people who are attempting to change a problem, such as ceasing to abuse alcohol, and are commonly led by a peer user, while support groups tend to be for people adapting to a problem, such as caring for a relative experiencing dementia, and are often led by a professional (not necessarily qualified in counselling or group work). The therapeutic factors outlined under counsellor-led groups, above, are also very much in evidence in self-help and support groups, although different clusters may be more prominent.

As already noted, self-help and support groups are not mutually exclusive, and the definition of a self-help group given by Richardson and Goodman is equally applicable to support groups: 'groups of people who feel they have a common problem . . . and have joined together to do something about it' (1983: 2). Self-help groups may be led by a particular peer leader, may be leaderless or may have a rotating leader, but Lew has suggested that it is 'very helpful to have a leader' (1993: 216).

Support groups have been formed for people disabled by the following (Nichols and Jenkinson, 1991: 8–9):

- arthritis
- mastectomy
- colostomy
- severe burns
- heart failure and heart attack
- multiple sclerosis
- infertility
- spinal injury
- head injury
- amputation
- tinnitus
- severe skin disorder
- AIDS

and for people exposed to the distress of others or carrying heavy burdens of care and responsibility, such as (Nichols and Jenkinson, 1991: 8–9):

- parents of children with cancer
- parents of children who die
- parents of brain-damaged children
- partners of people surviving by dialysis
- partners of people who have had a heart attack
- family care-givers for those with senile and pre-senile dementia
- family care-givers for those with progressive neurological diseases
- family care-givers for those with strokes.

Self-help groups have been formed for people who experience difficulties with the following:

- alcohol dependency
- gambling
- depression
- post-natal depression
- eating disorders
- being survivors of sexual abuse.

This is not a comprehensive list, and groups will not necessarily be available in your geographical area. The therapeutic factors noted above are the main benefits of self-help and support groups, but education and training are important minor elements. Groups exist in which education and training are the main focus, such as assertiveness, stress management and relaxation training, which are usually led by a professional.

It is not uncommon, in assessing a person with psychological difficulties, to discover that she is overwhelmed with a variety of problems, some of which may require expert advice. Common examples are legal difficulties, financial problems, confusion over social security benefits, housing troubles, violent or noisy neighbours and so on. The Citizens' Advice Bureaux offer a good source of advice about a wide range of problems and can sometimes arrange for free expert advice if necessary. The local council offers advice about the services it controls, including environmental health. Some neighbourhoods operate law centres offering free legal advice. There are also a growing number of helplines listed at the front of the *Yellow Pages* and local telephone directories, offering both practical advice (such as help with benefits) and emotional support (such as the Samaritans and Saneline).

When clients are so overwhelmed with practical problems that they are failing to cope with them, and their mental health is suffering, it may be helpful to guide them to their general practitioner who will be able to access a range of social services.

Practice Point

An individual may benefit from a self-help group or support group. This may be in addition to, or instead of counselling. Discuss with your client.

Conclusion

This chapter has considered what type of help is available to people with psychological problems. It is best read in conjunction with Chapter 5 which discusses therapeutic orientation. Some of the options presented may not be available locally for the people you assess, and it will be beneficial for you to acquaint yourself with the services available in your immediate and surrounding areas. The various options outlined above are rarely absolutely mutually exclusive, and where, for example, a preferred approach is unavailable (such as family therapy) an alternative can usually offer some success but may require the counsellor to work creatively.

References

Ackerman, N. (1966) *Treating the Troubled Family*. New York: Basic Books.

Bloch, S. (1986) 'Supportive psychotherapy', in S. Bloch (ed.), *An Introduction to the Psychotherapies* (2nd edn). Oxford: Oxford University Press.

Bloch, S. (1988) 'Research in group psychotherapy', in M. Aveline and W. Dryden (eds), *Group Therapy in Britain*. Milton Keynes: Open University Press.

Brown, G.W. and Birley, J.L.T. (1968) 'Crises and life changes and the onset of schizophrenia', *Journal of Health and Social Behaviour*, 9: 203–41.

Budman, S.H. and Gurman, A.S. (1988) *Theory and Practice for Brief Therapy*. New York: Guilford.

Caplan, G. (1961) *An Approach to Community Mental Health*. London: Tavistock.

Crowe, M. and Ridley, J. (1990) *Therapy with Couples*. London: Blackwell Scientific Publications.

Davanloo, H. (ed.) (1978) *Basic Principles and Techniques in Short-Term Dynamic Psychotherapy*. New York: S.P. Medical and Scientific Books.

Dryden, W. (1995) *Brief Rational Emotive Behaviour Therapy*. Chichester: Wiley.

Dryden, W. and Feltham, C. (1994) *Developing the Practice of Counselling*. London: Sage.

Ellis, A. (1963) 'Towards a more precise definition of "emotional" and "intellectual" insight', *Psychological Reports*, 13: 125–6.

Ellis, A. (1996) *Better, Deeper and More Enduring Brief Therapy*. New York: Brunner/Mazel.

Falloon, I.R.H., Boyd, J.F. and McGill, C.W. (1984) *Family Care of Schizophrenia*. New York: Guilford Press.

Howard, K.I., Kopta, S.M., Krause, M.S. and Orlinsky, D.E. (1986) 'The dose–effect relationship in psychotherapy', *American Psychologist*, 41: 159–64.

Jacobson, N.S. and Gurman, A.S. (eds) (1995) *Clinical Handbook of Couple Therapy*. New York: Guilford Press.

Kaufman, E. and Kaufman, P. (eds) (1981) *Family Therapy of Drug and Alcohol Abuse*. New York: Gardner Press.

University of Nottingham
School of Nursing & Midwifery
Derbyshire Royal Infirmary
London Road
DERBY DE1 2QY

Kingdom, D.G. and Turkington, D. (1991) *Cognitive-Behavioural Therapy of Schizophrenia*. Hove: Lawrence Erlbaum.

Lazarus, L.W. (1982) 'Brief psychotherapy of narcissistic disturbance', *Psychotherapy: Theory, Research, Practice*, 35: 257–64.

Lew, M. (1993) *Victims No Longer*. London: Cedar.

Liebovitch, M. (1983) 'Why short-term psychotherapy for borderlines?', *Psychotherapy and Psychosomatics*, 39: 1–9.

Lindemann, E. (1944) 'Symptomatology of acute grief', *American Journal of Psychiatry*, 101: 141–8.

Malan, D.H. (1979) *Individual Psychotherapy and the Science of Psychodynamics*. Cambridge: Butterworths.

Malan, D.H. (1980) 'Criteria for selection', in H. Davanloo (ed.), *Short-Term Dynamic Psychotherapy*. New York: Jason Aronson.

Miller, W. and Rollnick, S. (eds) (1991) *Motivational Interviewing*. New York: Guilford Press.

Minuchin, S. (1974) *Families and Family Therapy*. London: Tavistock.

Minuchin, S., Rosman, B.L. and Baker, L. (1978) *Psychosomatic Families. Anorexia Nervosa in Context*. Harvard: Harvard University Press.

Nichols, K. and Jenkinson, J. (1991) *Leading a Support Group*. London: Chapman and Hall.

O'Farrell, T.J. (ed.) (1994) *Treating Alcohol Problems*. New York: Guilford Press.

Parry, G. (1992) 'Improving psychotherapy services: application of research audit and evaluation', *British Journal of Clinical Psychology*, 31 part 1: 3–19.

Richardson, A. and Goodman, M. (1983) *Self-Help and Social Care: Mutual Aid Organisations in Practice*. London: Policy Studies Institute.

Rosenfield, M. (1996) *Telephone Counselling*. London: Sage.

Schwarz, R.C. (1994) *Internal Family Systems Therapy*. New York: Guilford Press.

Shapiro, R.J. (1980) 'Psychodynamically orientated family therapy', in G.P. Sholevar, R. Benson and B. Blinder (eds), *Treatment of Emotional Disorders in Childhood and Adolescence*. Spectrum.

Shapiro, R.J. (1986) 'Alcohol and family violence', in L. Barnhill (ed.), *Clinical Approaches to Family Violence*. Aspen Systems.

Shapiro, R.J. (1988) 'Marital therapy', in H.H. Goldman (ed.), *Review of General Psychiatry* (2nd edn). London: Prentice-Hall. p. 559.

Wile, D.B. (1993) *After The Fight*. New York: Guilford Press.

Winston, A., Pollack, J., McCullough, L., Flegenheimer, W., Kestenbaum, W. and Trujillo, M. (1991) 'Brief psychotherapy of borderline disorders', *Journal of Nervous and Mental Disease*, 179: 188–93.

5 *Assessing for Optimal Therapeutic Intervention*

Mark Aveline

What Does the Client Want and Need?

With What Issues Does the Client Want Help?
The phone rings, a letter of referral or self-introduction arrives, an appointment for assessment is kept, contact has been made. The other, as yet in the role of an inquirer but potentially a client or patient, *may* be in need of help; but what it is that they want help with, and what kind of help if any is appropriate, has yet to be determined. I emphasise the conditional, as seeking help is neither the same as needing it nor the same as finding it in the first instance. This is where assessment has to begin with an open mind on the part of the counsellor, a readiness to enter into another's world, and a professional determination to do a good job either in person or by referring on. Skill, self-knowledge, wide knowledge of life, the capacity to observe what goes on in the assessment and to make hypotheses about the clinical significance of observations, and a professional attitude are all necessary attributes that the counsellor brings to the difficult, important task of assessment.

Let us begin with the time-honoured opening question: 'Where would you like to begin?' The question implies that not everything has to be spilled out incontinently: secrets can be reserved for when trust has been earned by the counsellor, and the starting point is set by the client. The client is in control but is also responsible for what is put forward for exploration – a position of discomfort when some simply want to be told what to do, others want not to reflect on their situation, and yet others are coming to placate a third party.

Once an opening has been made for the client to begin, an exercise in cartography is started, a map of the client's psychological world, jointly drawn by the participants in the assessment. What are the features of the terrain, what direction is the client taking in her life, what direction would she like to take, what obstacles obstruct the present path, are these obstacles self-made or constructed by others, and if the latter, by whom?

Remember that the map, however complete it may appear, is always partial. Quite properly, people do not immediately tell all that there is to tell; indeed, if they do, this may indicate a degree of recklessness that is of diagnostic significance and may point to previous abusive experiences that have reduced that person's capacity to take due care of themselves. I do not want here to impute pathological significance to the helpful, necessary and willing collaboration that enables the client to set out his world and which underpins the work of counselling and psychotherapy; rather, I want to indicate that in the drawing of the client's world, the counsellor needs to observe and interpret the emerging terrain. How the client manifests himself as a person is as important as the content of what he says. A further reason for the map being partial is that some localities are not in conscious awareness, though their presence and probable form may be deduced by a counsellor who is attuned to that level, and where their emergence into consciousness is a function of the therapeutic process. More simply, the act of telling and retelling alters what is told. Perspectives change with the perceived meaning of experience wherein perception is as much a function of meaning as it is of fact. It is in this possible recasting of the landscape that the benefit of the explorative therapies lie.

Mary, a woman in her 20s, was referred with a history of anorexia and depression. She had long, crimped hair; it spread from her head over her shoulders, filling the gap so that it was hard to see where she started and stopped. One might say that her appearance simply reflected fashion and was without further meaning. Yet her appearance paralleled her anguished silence and difficulty in starting to say what she wanted help with. I took her appearance as a statement which expressed her position in life and commented that it was hard for her to be seen by me. It transpired that she mostly did not want to be seen as a person, a habitual defence against being found boring and critically attacked as she had been in childhood. However, she came to ask for help because a small part of her hated her isolation, envied the attention that the more forthright secured and was prepared to risk being seen if that might help. The concept of being seen or not seen immediately defined part of her psychological landscape and was used by us as a grid reference in our conversation.

Is What Is Wanted Relevant to Therapy, within the Range of Effectiveness? Is This Something with which Therapy Can Help?

'How can I help you?' and 'What would you like help with?' are two similar questions. The former signals the counsellor's willingness to assist but implies an ability that has yet to be determined and, hence, in the sequence of assessment comes after the second question. Assessment has to determine what the client wants and if this is something with which the counsellor can both properly and practically help.

What Does the Client Need?

What clients need may be both different from and more than what they want. This might appear an arrogant statement but it is not intended as such. Consider Tom's case.

Tom's manager was concerned about his deteriorating work performance and suggested that he consult the confidential staff counselling service. The manager knew that Tom's wife had recently left him and wondered if he was depressed. On one occasion, Tom had failed to turn up for his shift as a bus driver, a most unusual event.

A dishevelled man in his late 30s, Tom told the counsellor that he suffered from indigestion and hand shaking, especially in the mornings. Otherwise, he maintained, there was nothing he was worried about; he was only attending to pacify the manager. On prompting, he admitted to having been in a fight though he had no recollection of what had happened. The shrewd counsellor asked him about his alcohol intake. 'This is not a problem,' Tom replied, 'though I am drinking a bottle of spirits a day. It's under control!'

The counsellor was not impressed by the reply and probed further. Tom admitted that, once he started drinking, he could not stop. Furthermore, life had no purpose now that he was alone; he felt betrayed by his wife who had left him for a colleague from work. He felt ashamed of the break-up and was reluctant to go into detail. The future was bleak. He was not managing his money, leaving bills unpaid and spending more than he could afford on alcohol. Noting the history of increasing alcohol intake, loss of control (over both alcohol and impulse), blackouts, tremor and gastritis, the counsellor diagnosed alcoholism in a depressed, previously competent man who was failing to come to terms with the major psychological loss of his marriage.

Tom identified indigestion and hand shaking as the main problems; he wanted them to be the focus and shied away from psychological exploration. The counsellor identified many more problems but the foremost of these was the alcoholism, especially as this was putting at risk not only Tom's health but also bus passengers and passers-by, people to whom the counsellor now has a duty of care since it had become known that they are at risk of harm. Tom's need is wider in scope than his want. This issue is explored in the next sub-section.

Levels of Problem

Problems vary in their (1) complexity, (2) level, (3) interconnect-edness, (4) degree of discomfort or disturbance that they create and (5) priority. In Tom's case, physical symptoms were his presenting and preferred level. Yet they were only one part of his terrain. The counsellor could see that they stood on a summit whose base was constructed from excess alcohol intake. Tom could not see that his symptoms stood on this base; he lacked *insight* into the significance of the link, a necessary perspective in securing consent to a counselling plan. Around the base is a desert, a barren land that, formerly and recently, had been fruitful. No tracks cross the desert. There is little to sustain life, either for Tom or for others. On the horizon in the direction of the past, the land is varied and peopled. The way forward is unclear. When driving his bus, Tom was a heavy monolith whose movement might crush those in his path.

In this case, levels of problem and priority are the same. In addressing Tom's needs, the rule of thumb is twofold: (1) start with the most urgent need, and (2) work from the superficial to the deeper, more complex problems. Tom is dependent on alcohol to a serious degree. At work, he is not coping and may be putting members of the public at risk when he drives. The counsellor needs to ensure that Tom does not drive until his alcoholism has been treated. Financially, his world is falling apart. He needs help to arrange his affairs, lest a collapse at this level compounds his difficulties. At the next level, he is depressed. This was triggered by the breakup of his marriage but may now be so severe as to amount to a clinical depression which could be helped by medication. The counsellor will need to consider referral for psychiatric evaluation (see Chapter 3). At the next level is the nature of Tom's marriage, its meaning in his life and the reasons for its end (if it has died). Is there scope for couple intervention? Beyond that lies the level of personal dynamics. What kind of a person is he, what contribution did he make to the marriage's demise, and what can he learn beneficially from the experience? How may he lead his life in the future?

Understanding

Clients are human beings leading their lives and having to grapple with the many internal and external changes, desired or imposed, that are an inevitable part of being alive. How people engage with the sequence of change depends on how they see the world and the inherent severity of the change. To a greater or lesser extent, the counsellor is continuously engaged in the task of teasing out the personal meaning that events have for the client. The counsellor may call upon systems of understanding which may be from psychodynamic, humanistic, existential, systems or learning theory to structure a deep understanding of the client and help answer the important question: *why is this person reacting to this situation in this way?* In my work, I draw on all these systems, emphasising the understanding that has the greatest explanatory power and, if possible, that is most intelligible to the individual in front of me. I incline particularly to psychodynamic understanding in making a formulation as this is a rich source, encompassing as it does the concept of intrapsychic conflict, repetition and development over the life-cycle.

What Challenges Are Being Faced in the Client's Life?
Change is an inevitable part of life. Many people might like to
avoid facing the reality of their situation but this can only be done
by simple avoidance, the conscious use of the mental mechanism
of suppression and the unconscious use of denial or one of its
variants that reduce the experience of anxiety through distortion
of perception. Despite the use of defence mechanisms, life proceeds apace with problems and their unresolved consequences
exerting their effect unless the fortuitous operation of chance or
the action of others dictates a solution. The counsellor has an
opportunity to assist the client in facing the challenges in that
person's life. The first step is to identify what these are. It is
helpful to place challenges in a development perspective.

A Developmental Perspective
Erik Erikson died in 1994. He trained as a psychoanalyst in Vienna
in the 1920s before moving to the United States where he taught
and practised on the eastern seaboard. Informed by his cultural
and clinical studies, he supplemented Freud's biological model of
development with a psychosocial dimension, identifying eight
stages in the whole life-cycle and introducing the concept of
'identity crisis', a clinically significant occurrence in late adolescence and early adulthood. Implicit in his epigenetic chart of
development (see Figure 5.1) is the idea of phase-specific
psychosocial tasks which optimally need to be engaged with and
completed at the appropriate time *and* which lay the foundation
for subsequent tasks.

   Thus in the first year of life, the task is to develop the capacity of
'basic trust'. The infant is totally dependent on others for physical
and emotional nurture. How that absolute need is responded to in
terms of quickness, appropriateness and reliability forms the
template for trust, what that individual can expect from others in
meeting their needs. In the second and third year of life, the child's
horizon expands. Able to explore and manipulate the environment, the child acquires a sense of self, separate from others.
Small experiences of separation from parents and experimentation
are necessary, risky events where failures can easily render the
child afraid and prone to self-doubt, shame and guilt. In contrast,
successful navigation of the stage results in the capacity to act
autonomously and sets the scene for the development of initiative.
This description gives but a taste of the full scheme. Readers are

8   Integrity vs despair

7   Generativity vs stagnation

6   Intimacy vs isolation

5   Identity vs identity confusion

4   Industry vs inferiority

3   Initiative vs guilt

2   Autonomy vs shame and doubt

1   Trust vs mistrust

Figure 5.1   *Epigenetic chart of development (Erikson, 1965)*

referred to Erikson's (1965: Chapter 7) original account or the book by Rayner (1986).

Humans have a biology but they express their humanity in social interaction. Their ability, in Harry Guntrip's words, 'to live life to the full in ways that enable us to realise our own natural potentialities, and that unite us with rather than divide us from all the other human beings who make up our world' (1964: 25) depends crucially on the successful learning of two essential human abilities that I have just described, namely a sufficient ability to trust others and to act independently. It is only through the exercise of these two abilities that maturity, a state defined by Fairbairn (1954), an original thinker in British object relations theory and Guntrip's mentor, as 'mature dependence', can be achieved.

The sequence of development over the life-cycle means that the developmental tasks of early years are revisited and there is opportunity for later learning of what has not been learnt fully before. In this way, beneficial learning can offset adverse past learning. Counselling and psychotherapy can be a source of new learning. Equally, later tasks become harder if a person's foundation is shaky. Thus the challenge of adolescence and young adulthood is, first, to develop a sense of individual identity and, second, to be intimate with a partner. Both tasks depend on the basic capacities of trust and autonomy. Someone whose basic attitude is one of suspicion will find it hard to risk the experiments in living in which the more fortunate engage, however anxiously. Similarly, someone whose individuality has not been recognised and whose achievements have not been valued will be more vulnerable to identity confusion.

Let us consider Tom's case developmentally.

Tom was the precious only child of his mother. His preciousness was underscored by his mother conceiving him in her 30s after many failed attempts and raising him in the general absence of his father, a sailor who materialised in the home every few months, disrupting its harmony through his drinking and irritated attempts to establish his presence. Mother and son were a source of mutual comfort. As a young child, Tom was shy and suffered from stomach cramps, often worsened by attending school; at such times, his mother frequently kept him home, a practice that his father criticised for not being manly. His parents split up when he was 12 and Tom lived on with his mother into his late 20s. He felt comfortable with his mother but outside the home lacked confidence in general and as a man. Aged 29, he married Linda, a long-standing girlfriend, five years older than himself.

The points to notice are Tom's close relationship with his mother which compensated her for deficiencies in the marriage, the absence of a satisfactory male figure with whom to identify, and a low level of autonomy as evidenced by his delayed separation from the parental home.

An Interactive Perspective

Until his wife left him, Tom existed within a stable context of marriage and work. Let us examine the interactive pattern of the marriage, as it was the removal of this cornerstone that brought down the edifice of his life.

Linda was the eldest in a family of four, her siblings all being male. The family was close and needed to be as her father was progressively incapacitated by emphysema, aggravated by incessant smoking. When Linda was eight, her mother died in a car accident and she assumed the role of care-giver. Her father depended on her to keep him and the family going and appreciated all that she did. In her teens, she forwent the chance to go to university, an opportunity that two of her brothers took up. She took part-time work. At the age of 32, her father's death was a great blow. She had known Tom for several years, their relationship being a low-key one. In the aftermath of her father's death, the relationship intensified and they married. Tom appreciated Linda's care and attention and, for a while, Linda was comfortable in what was an extension of her previous life. Tom visited his mother every day. He worked diligently and looked to Linda to order his life. They had no children.

People tend to repeat formative patterns of interaction. Unconsciously, they look for others to play complementary roles in learnt dramas. These learnt dramas represent attempts at adaptation at a particular formative stage, though the result is often maladaptive in the longer term. Later in life, problems may arise when either the pattern damages current relationships or other key players cease to be content with their role. The latter is what happened with Tom.

Caring for Tom was a familiar role for Linda. It had the rightness of long usage but this sense of rightness had been bought at the price of denial of individual needs and an under-development of individuality. She was saddened by not having children. Thinking of Tom as a child was no compensation. In her late 30s, she began to question the pattern of her life. She worked for the same bus company as Tom, an arrangement which lacked originality but which provided a common point of reference as well as being a necessary part of the family finances. Here her horizons expanded through work in the union; she met Hugh, the man for whom she left Tom. They shared political interests and she started to think of herself as someone who could have a larger role in society than wife and employee. Her frustrated wish to study was rekindled, perhaps through being a mature student at university. Linda and Tom's paths began to diverge, introducing a challenge of adaptation into their marriage that proved too great for them to surmount.

Tom reacted defensively to the flowering of her ambitions by opposing change and trying to reinstate the old pattern of dependence and mothering. Guiltily, Linda faced the consequences of realising that she had one life to live, the strength of her wish to be creative (Erikson's seventh stage) and the limitations of her relationship with her husband; and then she left. Tom felt betrayed by the abandonment of an implicit bargain which once had been all that either had wanted and where he had continued to play his part, even though the plot had changed.

Levels of Problem Revisited

We can now revisit the issue of levels of problem and consider the final question of personal dynamics. What kind of a person is

Tom, what contribution did he make to the marriage's demise, and what can he learn beneficially from the experience? How may he lead his life in the future? In the preceding sections, we have seen how the definition of the problem broadened from a narrow one of physical symptoms to a wider perspective once his developmental progress and psychosocial context were considered. We can name the significant elements in the problematic matrix of his life. The interaction is between the stress (his marriage unravelling), his development (arrested at a dependent stage) and his context (a marriage where mutuality had been replaced by unbridgeable divergence); the consequence is an attempted solution of stasis and alcoholic oblivion. This interactive matrix helps explain *why is he reacting to this situation in this way*.

Doubtless other explanations have validity. This formulation is supported by the evidence of the case and is sufficiently plausible for Tom and the counsellor to use it to make sense of his problems, understand their probable genesis, and make a therapy plan. Part of making a plan is knowing what the therapies can achieve, an expert contribution by the counsellor to the planning debate. This is the focus of the next section. Before moving to that focus, take time to reflect on what Tom might have to face up to in explorative counselling or psychotherapy.

Tom has already shown that he wants to take a restricted view of his problems. Reflecting on his contribution to the marriage's demise is going to be hard. He is full of rage and sees himself as the victim of betrayal. He is ashamed of losing Linda to a colleague. He wants to be revenged but, for the most part, takes his anger out on himself, ending up depressed and alcohol dependent. He is bewildered by the unforeseen change of direction in his life and is ill-equipped through past experience to cope with the new demands ahead. In therapy, he would have to face the way his dependence held back the development of the marriage to the point where it fractured. He would be faced with a choice of continuing as he is, hoping to find another partner with similar symbiotic needs, or attempting to change in the direction of greater autonomy and differentiation as a person. This is not an impossible task but it would be hard work. Truly, there are no easy rides in any therapy that is challenging. Only in retrospect might he judge the learning beneficial.

Practice Points

Keep an open mind.

Begin to jointly map the client's world.

Tease out levels of problems.

Don't be afraid to tell the truth as you see it as part of the negotiation.

In telling the truth, bear in mind the importance of timing and what the client can bear to hear.

Don't assume that consultation is a mandate for therapy.

Place challenges in a development and interactive perspective.

Derive a formulation from the evidence:

- what is said and not said
- how it is said (verbal, non-verbal and enactments of relationship patterns)
- what you feel during the assessment (counter-transference)
- your knowledge of psychological processes and development.

Knowing What the Therapies Can Achieve and Their Limitations

The Hierarchy of Intervention from Advice, Guidance and Counselling to Psychotherapy

Interventions vary in their therapeutic scope, appropriateness and degree of required sustained commitment by the client. Generalising, advice and guidance are brief task-centred interventions over one, two or three sessions. Information is often given and the client may be pointed in the direction of other expert resources in employment, welfare rights and services, and legal practice. The counsellor will commonly have special training in the area of activity such as education or business for which advice or guidance is being given. The focus is circumscribed and definitely practical.

In counselling and psychotherapy, the focus is less circumscribed; the outcome may be more intangible, though still of practical benefit. Certainly, counselling and psychotherapy require a much greater degree of sustained commitment by the client. The number of therapy sessions may vary from six to ten as in most employee assistance programmes (EAPs) and in counselling in general practice in the NHS, to brief focused psychotherapies of 16 to 25 sessions as in cognitive-analytic therapy (CAT) (Ryle, 1990), to individual or group therapies at weekly or more intensive frequencies over one to three or more years. The therapeutic aims range on a spectrum with at least five increments: (1) relieving pent-up feelings through facilitating the telling of the client's story, (2) enabling that person to face her situation, consider choices and make decisions, (3) promoting understanding of the personal meanings of events and the complexity and contradictory nature of motivations, (4) the identification of recurrent, maladaptive patterns of interaction and thought and (5) change in these self-restrictive patterns. The counselling process facilitates the assumption of personal responsibility for that part of life for which the individual can properly be responsible and the exercise of free will through choice.

Short- and Long-Term Therapy

In achieving the aims of therapy at a point on the above spectrum, duration, frequency and technique are three important factors. Howard, a psychologist, therapist and researcher from Northwestern University in Chicago, has demonstrated three phases in his *dosage model* of psychotherapeutic effectiveness: (1) remoralization, (2) remediation and (3) rehabilitation (Howard et al., 1995). The phases occur in sequence and each is a prelude to the next. Different disorders such as anxiety or borderline personality disorder show distinct patterns of timing of phases in response to psychotherapy but, overall, greater dosage of therapy is needed to achieve the second phase and, certainly, the third.

In the beginning, the patient is demoralised by his problems, often to the point where he is not able to use their personal coping resources. Simply being offered an appointment for assessment may sufficiently reduce distress that the patient can begin to cope again in his usual way. Alternatively, *remoralization* may occur through the general therapeutic factors of interest, support and relief from stress in the first few therapy sessions. This may be enough for some. Others will enter the second phase of *remediation* in which, through the development of insight and the use of cognitive and behavioural strategies over three to four months (around 16 sessions), coping skills are refocused to bring about symptomatic relief. The period may be longer or shorter. Again, remediation may be sufficient for some but others will have gained a deeper understanding of themselves wherein they can see that both problems and patterns of solution are recurrent and maladaptive and will want to unlearn old patterns and relearn less self-restrictive patterns of interaction. This is the stuff of explorative therapy. The period of *rehabilitation* may last months or years depending on the accessibility and malleability of the maladaptive patterns.

While I do not greatly care for Howard's terms, the implications of the research are clear. In principle, what longer-term therapy delivers is different from what can be achieved in the short term. Character change takes time – and commitment – and requires skill on the part of the therapist. Not everyone wants or needs character change (rehabilitation) and that is their decision. But the process of therapy helps some people realise that they have to change themselves in order to change the way that they engage with life.

Individual, Group, Couple and Family Therapy

Therapies have specific effects and aptitudes. Individual counselling affords psychological space and time to explore personal history and individual problems. Intensity in terms of both depth and speed can be fine-tuned to individual need. Cognitive-behavioural work fits naturally with those whose perspective is limited to symptoms and who want to be directed in their therapy. In addition, cognitive-behavioural therapy has a clear advantage in research trials in the treatment of phobias, bulimia and obsessive compulsive disorder (Hollen and Beck, 1994).

Couple, group and family therapy introduces another theoretical dimension in the form of the system. What happens in a group of people is a product of the whole group with each member influencing the others and the sum being more than the constituent parts. Crucially, change in one part of the system affects the whole system. Thus, clients may be stuck in interactive patterns that can only be freed up by engaging the key other. Couple work addresses a living relationship wherein people show their strengths and vulnerabilities and play out their conflicts. Change achieved here has an immediate benefit. The same is true of family therapy. In the artificial creation of group therapy, stranger groups provide a splendid setting in which the client can learn about how he or she interacts, sees others and is seen. It is a laboratory in which risks can be taken and change made. In addition, groups can provide a supportive 'family' for clients with long-term needs and dilute the impact of those whose paranoia, fragility or dependence would be overwhelming in individual counselling. Further guidance on assessing for particular types of therapy is to be found in Mace (1995).

The Location of the Problem

Where the problem is located helps to decide the therapy. The location may be within the individual psyche (intrapsychic) or between the client and others (interpersonal). Intrapsychic problems and problematic attitudes to self which do not involve another person in a current intimate relationship or where that other person is unwilling to be involved suggest individual therapy. When the problem is located within a particular relationship such as a couple and that is the problem that the client wants to resolve, focus the therapy on the couple. Group counselling is indicated for recurrent, maladaptive relationship patterns or where an important therapeutic element of the counselling is sharing some experience in common, such as cancer, sexual abuse, phobias and eating disorder. Self-help groups reduce the sense of isolation and provide a forum for peer support. This distinction between intrapsychic and interpersonal is not absolute; it is an indicative predominance. The same point is made in the next sub-section.

The Interactive Relationship between Inner and Outer Worlds

An artificial distinction is sometimes drawn between the inner psychological world of thought, emotion and conflict and the external world of action and its underpinnings in conscious thought and feeling. While there are real differences between psychodynamic and cognitive-behavioural counselling and psychotherapy, the two are sometimes pitted as polar opposites, thereby encouraging a fight to the death in which political advantage in the form of employment and training school supremacy is the winner and clients the losers. Psychodynamic psychotherapy takes as its perspective the past and the present with particular emphasis on relationships, their form and formation. The approach is an inner one, attending as it does to unconscious processes and intrapsychic and interpersonal conflicts which are enacted in the *transference* and may be resolved in that therapy space. Cognitive-behavioural counselling and psychotherapy focus on the present and future with particular emphasis on symptoms, their origins in faulty logic and maintenance by external reinforcers of behaviour. Restrictive patterns of thought and behaviour are disrupted by dispute and by homework and *in vivo* practice, directively set and systematically reviewed.

On principle, I disapprove of the few psychodynamic therapies that go nowhere despite being intense (consuming resources that someone else might benefit from) and cognitive-behavioural therapies that are reductionist and bullying. That said, I take an open-handed stance, wanting the best for the client. The acid test of therapy is change in the real world, and either an inner or an outer approach can help. Both influence how a person approaches their life and shapes their future. The approaches, however, make different appeals to client and therapist alike.

The Client's Orientation and Preference

Client orientation and preference need to be given due weight in choosing a therapy. Some clients do not want to dwell on underlying processes and prefer to be directed in taking therapeutic action. Brevity and tangible action will appeal. They will be drawn to the cognitive-behavioural approach. Others want to understand their processes, set these in their historical context and, through exploration, relieve the pressure of the past on the present. They will want time to come to terms with events, to make life decisions and develop the courage to act. Their preference may be for a psychodynamic approach. For similar reasons, therapists will be drawn to either orientation. Another group of clients may want to focus on their inner resources, choosing their own way forward with little counsellor direction or influence. Such clients may prefer a person-centred approach.

Giving due weight in choosing a therapy to client preference does not mean that preference is an absolute imperative. It means working with the grain when this is appropriate. Just as *not* accepting the limitation of perspective that Tom wanted to impose (in the case example) is one aspect of professional responsibility in assessment, another is challenging the client's preference when there is evidence that the expressed wish represents a flight from the optimal therapeutic task. Discomfort with feelings and intimate relationships may prompt the choice of the typically more rational, less messy cognitive-behavioural approach when greater benefit could accrue from psychodynamic work. Conversely, the client may be evading introducing change into his or her life by opting for the perceived relative timelessness and non-directive-ness of psychodynamic or person-centred counselling. As I argued earlier, it is a question of assessing what a person needs as well as what they want. Exploring the reasons for the preference and how that person has responded to any prior exposure to therapy elucidates the question.

The Counsellor's Talents

Many factors meld together in producing the outcome of therapy. Within the world of the counselling session, these include the type and severity of problems, the client's personality and motivation, the appropriateness and intrinsic power of the therapy, and the skill, motivation and healing capacity of the counsellor. The last plays a major part in realising the therapeutic promise of the deployed approach. Just as the client's part is to reflect on their situation, so is the counsellor's to be realistic about their ability and be prepared to refer on when that is in the client's best interest.

Practice Points

Be aware of the strengths and weaknesses of the different therapies.

Work out where the problem is predominantly located.

Appreciate the interactive relationship between a person's inner and outer worlds.

Take account of client preference for type of intervention.

Be realistic about what one can provide.

Putting Together a Package That Is Right for the Client (as Right as One Can Know)

Tailoring Intervention to Individual Need and Want

Clients turn to counsellors to obtain help, support or expertise. In tailoring intervention to individual need and want, there are two necessary prior processes, namely finding out what the client wants and needs and knowing what the therapies can achieve; these have been considered in the previous sections. It is not enough to simply know the indications and contra-indications of the different therapies. Benefit from intervention is not determined purely by type of therapy but is the product of a complex and uncertain interaction between the form and severity of problems, the client's personality, developmental stage and motivation, the appropriateness and intrinsic power of the therapy, the skill, motivation and healing capacity of the counsellor, the malleability of the life situation and the operation of chance and good or ill fortune.

The following principles inform the choice of intervention. The first two are conservative in the sense of keeping entire and are of primary importance.

Minimum Interventions

Problems vary in their complexity, level and interconnectedness, the degree of discomfort or disturbance that they create, and their priority. As we saw earlier with Tom's case, the rule of thumb is to start with the most urgent need, and work from the superficial to the deeper, more complex problems. Above all, do the minimum necessary to enable movement to take place in the client's life. Counselling and psychotherapy are aids to life, not solutions or substitutes. The sooner therapy can enable the client to discover and use their strengths, the better.

Not Doing Harm

To do well in explorative therapy, a degree of flexibility is necessary. Leaving well alone may be the right course when the counsellor judges that the client's inner world is so fragile that any change would be for the worse or that the client has insufficient personal resources to make major developmental moves.

Jim, a lively and engaging man in his 60s, presented with intermittent severe anxiety and depression. These feelings were at variance with his usual and much preferred state of being the life and soul of any gathering and being helpful to others. His depressions were triggered by not being able to occupy these sustaining roles. At such times, indistinct memories of his childhood would surface from the obscurity of not being able to remember anything before the age of 10, in itself a probable, cautionary sign of a need to repress. In the assessment, I pressed him on the possible link between past and present. He spoke of everything being all right and, then, alarming 'cracks opening up'. His next association was to a memory as a child of being chased round a table by his stepfather with a knife and his mother not intervening. This was said to be a joke. I took this to have two meanings: first, that this was the tip of an iceberg of traumatic experiences; and, second, that his words were a process commentary on what was happening between us. He was warning me that my inquiry had the same feel as his stepfather's murderous 'game'. I interpreted his instruction to back off but he was unable to see the link and merely reported feeling uncomfortable.

His history gave further cause for concern. In his marriage, he looked to his wife for reassurance. Whenever he had a doubt, he would externalise it and, as it were, off-load it onto her for her to worry about. He could not bear to be upset. In the past, he had once been admitted to a psychiatric hospital with depression but this quickly worsened, I surmise, through being in a place where he was one of the distressed. His response was to discharge himself and work obsessively as a volunteer in a hospital casualty department.

Taking care is important. Jim's story is of someone who could not bear to be distressed and whose whole life had been built around avoiding that eventuality. It is likely that any explorative therapy would destabilise a generally successful adaptation and provoke further distress. Maintaining and reinforcing his defences was the best course.

Client's Ability to Enter into a Therapy Relationship

The client's ability to enter into a therapy relationship needs to be taken into account. I find Strupp and Binder's (1984) selection criteria helpful. The client should be *sufficiently discomforted* by their feelings or behaviour to seek help through counselling or psychotherapy, have *sufficient basic trust* in order to attend regularly and talk about their life, be *willing to consider conflicts in interpersonal terms*, be *willing to examine feelings* in the spirit that that activity might be helpful and relevant, and have *sufficient capacity for mature relationships* so that, when the conflicts are enacted in the therapy relationship, the client can allow them to be collaboratively examined. Strupp and Binder would exclude those who are so mistrustful or isolated that a *dynamic focus* cannot be defined or, if defined, where the process of definition is not perceived by the client as being meaningful or helpful; another related category are clients who are unable to perceive others as separate whole human beings. A final inclusion criterion is *motivation for the treatment* offered, judged by the developing ability of the client to relate to the therapist as a potentially helpful adult. No absolute level is set for each criterion, rather what is sought is a willingness to try.

Timing

Often there is an *auspicious time* (Greek *kairos*) in a person's life to take stock and alter established ways; counselling then may be especially helpful. Conversely, there are times when it is better to defer counselling or leave well alone. A case for deferment can be, for example, during pregnancy when the focus of the mother's attention is predominantly and necessarily inwards; raising major external questions during this period through therapy can significantly increase stress.

Informed Choice

In regard to timing, people do not develop in the way that they do by chance. A person's defences, however inappropriate and out of date they are now, were needed ways of coping with difficult situations in the past and should not be forced to yield, except as new strengths develop. The assessor has responsibility for gauging *potential gains and losses* through therapy and discussing these with the client so that he or she can make an *informed choice* about proceeding. Therapy frequently disrupts the status quo and in so doing opens the way to change, but the new state may not be acceptable to the parties concerned; the marriage, occupation, dependence on parents and balance of interests may all be questioned. One-off exploratory or trial sessions, particularly of individual therapy, can help the client make an informed choice.

Points of Leverage

Formulating a case will begin to identify the interactive matrix of the client's life. It will state who is involved and make some estimate of their contribution to the system. The formulation may highlight points of leverage where there is greater readiness to allow or make change. Thus as well as considering the location of the problem, explore with the client where to focus the therapy so that the chance of fostering movement is greatest.

Combined and Serial Therapy and Referring On

Consideration needs to be given to providing different forms of counselling in sequence and, in complex cases, referring on for more specialised therapy. For example, the optimum intervention might be a group but first the client might need to work through individually a particular aspect of her or his history or develop sufficient trust in order to be able to benefit from the sharing and exposure of a group.

Allow for Change of Goals over Time with Increased Understanding

How clients see the problem initially will nearly always be different from later on in therapy. Their view of the terrain will be enlarged and hidden aspects may become visible. The implication for the counsellor is to be vigilant and to reassess frequently where the intervention is going and could go.

Carl, a bright self-centred man whose working life had been devoted to the pursuit of scientific truth without consideration for the feelings of colleagues, wanted help in improving his relationships. He felt unable to read the reactions of others to him. As a member of a therapy group, he did indeed show himself to be unwilling to compromise on issues of principle and reluctant to sacrifice his desires for the benefit of others but he did not show himself to be insensitive to others as he had declared. On the contrary, he was unable to tolerate other members being distressed and would rush in with advice and solutions before the problem had properly been set out. This formulation of why he reacted as he did was a radically different change in perspective for him; it reversed the definition of the problem from insensitivity to over-sensitivity.

Does the Counsellor Have the Relevant Skills, Time and Interest?

Account should be taken of the interaction between the client's readiness to benefit and the complexity of problems, and the counsellor's compatibility and availability. There certainly needs to be matching on sufficient harmony of outlook and often there are advantages to match on age and sex. Beware of too great a similarity in life experience with the client. Some identification is essential but too much promotes over-identification and risks confusing the counsellor's personal issues with those of the client (Aveline, 1992).

If the counsellor is assessing for his or her own practice, the key question is: *do I have sufficient time, interest and relevant skills for the therapy of this client? If not, who has?* Time is important as ideally, once started, the counselling should be seen through to its conclusion. It is not ethical to open up major issues without providing space and time for resolution. Time for supervision is also important.

New Episodes, Sustenance and Reunions

Counselling does not exhaust the potential for adverse reactions to the problems that life throws up. Temper purity of therapy approach with pragmatism and humanity. Allow for the possibility of new episodes and consider offering reunion or follow-up meetings. These can help sustain the client.

Practice Points

Follow the twin primary principles of minimum intervention and not doing harm.

Work from simpler problems to the more complex.

Identify points of leverage.

Recognise that the client's goals change over time and with deepening insight.

Be flexible; different forms of therapy may be necessary at different stages.

Be realistic about one's own ability as a counsellor and what could be better offered by others.

Take care of the client.

Conclusion

The recommendation to clients of type of therapeutic intervention is not an exact science. Many suggestions for good practice have been made in this chapter; it will not be possible to realise all of them in every assessment. Assessment is an opportunity for a creative encounter between client and counsellor. The counsellor brings to the meeting expertise in assessment and therapy and the client brings his or her individual wants and needs. Assessment provides a taste of therapy and acts as an orientation to therapy. It is the beginning of what may prove to be a new beginning in the client's life.

References

Aveline, M.O. (1992) 'Parameters of danger: interactive elements in the therapy dyad', in M. Aveline (ed.), *From Medicine to Psychotherapy*. London: Whurr.

Erikson, E.E. (1965) *Childhood and Society*. Harmondsworth: Penguin.

Fairbairn, W.R.D. (1954) *An Object-Relations Theory of the Personality*. New York: Basic Books.

Guntrip, H.H. (1964) *Healing the Sick Mind*. London: Unwin.

Hollen, S.D. and Beck, A.T. (1994) 'Cognitive and cognitive-behavioral therapies', in A.L. Bergin and S.L. Garfield (eds), *Handbook of Psychotherapy and Behavior Change*. New York: Wiley. pp. 428–66.

Howard, K.I., Orlinsky, D.E. and Lueger, R.J. (1995) 'The design of clinically relevant outcome research: some considerations and examples', in M. Aveline and D. Shapiro (eds), *Research Foundations for Psychotherapy Practice*. London: Wiley.

Mace, C. (1995) *The Art and Science of Assessment in Psychotherapy*. London: Routledge.

Rayner, E. (1986) *Human Development* (3rd edn). London: Allen and Unwin.

Ryle, A. (1990) *Cognitive-Analytic Therapy: Active Participation in Change*. Chichester: Wiley.

Strupp, H.H. and Binder, J.L. (1984) *Psychotherapy in a New Key*. New York: Basic Books.

6 *Assessment and Accountability*

Patricia Armstrong

The concept of goal setting/attainment in counselling can evoke a response of trepidation, anxiety and negativity in many counsellors, in that its connotations of quantification are often seen as incompatible with the counselling process. Counselling is a stressful activity and introducing the idea of assessment and evaluation, which naturally results in the generation of even more work, almost inevitably results in counsellors resisting involvement.

Many counsellors in both the statutory and non-statutory sectors are under increasing pressure to provide outcome results that can be measured by fund-holders, and although counsellors may feel very uncomfortable with this prospect, goal setting may be a means of providing such a measure. 'Outcome' refers to changes that happen as a result of counselling and is typically measured as changes that occur between counselling assessment and final counselling session. This type of outcome potentially offers important feedback to the counsellor as well as clear evidence to clients, managers and fund-holders that the counsellor is taking evaluation seriously.

Reactions commonly put forward by counsellors when I have introduced goal attainment as a measure of outcome are:

1   incompatibility with the counselling process
2   meeting distress at a time of crisis with a request to set goals
3   time involved in analysing results
4   the most appropriate method for approaching clients.

Counsellors' misgivings need to be considered carefully when introducing the idea of any type of outcome measure in any organisation. However, a careful analysis of the above mentioned misgivings will serve to allay counsellors' fears. Goal setting is an integral part of many counselling approaches (for example cognitive-behavioural, Egan's model) and is therefore not a problem for counsellors working within these theoretical frameworks.

Goal setting in counselling can offer dual benefits in that clients can monitor their own tangible evidence of change, and counselling is based on the principle of enabling clients to achieve their potential within the limitations of their capabilities and environment.

Bordin (1979) has argued that goal setting is the *raison d'être* of the counselling process, and that goals pertain to the objectives both counsellor and client have for coming together in the alliance. Many have argued that a better therapeutic outcome is facilitated when the counsellor and client agree what the clients' goals are and agree to work towards the fulfilment of these goals. It may be argued that the therapeutic alliance is threatened when either explicitly, or more commonly implicitly, the counsellor and client have different outcome goals in mind for the client. Sutton (1989) suggests a means of overcoming this potential difficulty by advocating a written goal-setting agreement.

Dryden (1989) proposes that goal setting in counselling is of paramount importance in enabling the counsellor and client to build a mutual sense of 'therapeutic purpose'. One of Egan's (1995) main criticisms of the helping professions is that too many counsellors remain with clients in the initial exploratory phase, and fail to move them forward. This problem might well be resolved if counselling goals were made explicit in the initial assessment session.

What decision-making procedures should a counsellor follow to enable clients to reach realistic attainable goals? On the basis of the relevant research literature, the following six problem-solving procedures have been extracted as the basic ones for arriving at a sound decision (goal) (Janis and Mann, 1977):

1 Thoroughly canvass a wide variety of alternative courses of action.
2 Take account of the full range of objectives to be fulfilled and the values implicated by the choice.
3 Carefully weigh whether clients know about the costs or drawbacks and the uncertain risk of negative consequences as

well as the positive consequences that could flow from each alternative.

4 Intensively search for new information relevant to further evaluation of the alternatives.

5 Conscientiously take account of any new information or expert judgement to which the client is exposed.

6 Re-examine the positive and negative consequences of all known alternatives, including those originally regarded as unacceptable, before making a final choice.

According to Janis and Mann (1977) failure to meet any of these criteria is assumed to be a deficit in the decision-making process. It is argued that counsellors have a responsibility to adhere to the above mentioned steps when working with clients towards reaching a goal, as decisions that suffer from most or all of these defects generally have much less chance of success than those that do not. The more such defects are present before clients become committed, the greater are the chances that they will undergo unanticipated setbacks and post-decisional regret processes, that make for failure to reach the goal.

Practice Points

Be aware that you are not projecting your goals onto the client.

Make goals explicit.

Adhere to the criteria of the decision-making process.

What Are Goals?

Goals are defined by the Pelican *Dictionary of Psychology* (Reber, 1985) in the following straightforward way: 'the basic meaning is little different from that found in a standard dictionary in that in most usages some end result is implied'. Therefore, it seems reasonable to assume that counselling goals would be the purpose that both client and counsellor have for coming together, and if the goal is specific it can be seen as a quantifiable behavioural change over time.

But how do clients interpret the use of the word 'goals' in the counselling context? A recent pilot study requested clients to consider which of the following words they considered was user-friendly: 'goal' 'aim' 'target', or 'objective'. An overwhelming 87 per cent felt more comfortable with 'aim'. The use of the word 'goal' seemed to be too challenging for vulnerable clients (with connotations of winning, scoring, etc.), whereas the word 'aim' was viewed by clients as less threatening and intensive. This result may ultimately have an influence on the wording of outcome measures.

Setting Goals

Steve De Shazer (1986) suggests the following criteria in the development of well formed goals:

1   Goals should be small. Small goals are more easily achieved than large goals.
2   Well formed goals are salient to the client and viewed by the client as important.
3   Well formed goals must be concrete and defined in specific behavioural terms.
4   Goals need to be stated in the presence of something new and good, rather than the absence of something old and undesirable.
5   A well formed goal makes a statement about the start of something new and desirable rather than the end of something old and undesirable.
6   Well formed goals must be realistically attainable in the client's life situation.
7   The attainment of well formed goals must be viewed by the client as involving hard work.

Helping Clients To Set Goals

Brainstorming can be a component part of goal setting in counselling. This involves generating ideas which present various options, writing them down without comment. Quantity rather than quality is the initial idea. The next step is to combine and group the ideas and eventually evaluate them. For example, Jim, who recently divorced his wife and is attempting to rebuild his life as a single person, produced the following list of ideas:

■   be less isolated
■   develop a new social circle

- find new interests
- be more confident
- be more assertive
- learn new things
- further my education.

Given the above ideas, how might Jim arrive at what might be considered a realistic, attainable, measurable goal?

Force-Field Analysis
The counsellor might employ the analytic tool of force-field analysis to enable Jim to reach a realistic goal. A force-field analysis involves examining the factors that will enhance or inhibit Jim's ability to achieve his goal.

Restraining forces:

1 lack of confidence
2 lack of knowledge as to what is available
3 not knowing anyone
4 scared of new beginnings.

These restraining forces are definite indicators for the counsellor as to what the client might consider they are currently capable of achieving; hence the need for originally small attainable goals.

Facilitating forces:

1 available funding
2 desire to change
3 need to extend social circles
4 knowledge of resources available
5 time available
6 friends in similar position
7 peer/family influence.

The facilitating forces need to outweigh the restraining forces in setting realistic attainable goals. A careful analysis of the facilitating and restraining forces will assist both client and counsellor to determine goals that the client feels comfortable with.

Hierarchy of Human Needs Model

An additional useful analytic tool that might be employed in goal setting is Maslow's (1954) 'theory of sequential development'. It reminds counsellors that all clients' problems take place within the context of their environment and the ability to effect change will be influenced by many diverse factors, such as financial difficulties, environmental problems, and social situation.

Maslow suggests that the hierarchy of human needs model takes the form of a pyramid divided into seven groups, represented in the following way:

- *Group 1: physiological*   Hunger, thirst, air, rest, elimination of waste, sex.
- *Group 2: Safety*   Freedom from threat or danger, need to allay oneself with the safe, the familiar.
- *Group 3: belongingness and love*   Affiliation, identification with others, acceptance, affection.
- *Group 4: esteem*   Respect of others, self-respect, prestige, success, reputation, achievement.
- *Group 5: self-actualization*   To realise one's potentialities, become what one is capable of becoming (the desire for self-fulfilment).
- *Group 6: cognitive*   To know and understand, to tackle the unknown.
- *Group 7: aesthetic*   Structure system.

Maslow's hierarchy of human needs represents one version of the various stages that we progress through to achieve self-actualization. Maslow argues that needs lower down in the hierarchy must be satisfied before we can fully attend to the needs at the next level up: for example, physiological needs must be met before an individual can consider esteem needs.

If a client is setting goals higher up in the hierarchy, for example esteem needs, but has not worked through the lower needs, then according to Maslow the likelihood of meeting these goals is remote. For example, a single parent surviving on income support will be restricted by his/her living conditions. His/her living conditions and disposable income will limit the ability to effect change that might result in increased self-esteem. If when working with this client the goal agreed is greater self-esteem, and this goal is agreed without due consideration of practical financial and living conditions, then it might be an unrealistic goal for this particular client.

Therefore it is both useful and arguably necessary to consider Maslow's hierarchy of needs model when developing goals with clients.

Practice Points

Work towards setting small achievable goals.

Pay attention to clients' ambivalence.

Be aware of the facilitating/restraining forces.

Consider Maslow's hierarchy of human needs model.

What Do Clients Really Want?

Both Egan (1995) and Glasser (1989) place great emphasis on this question when helping clients to formulate goals, or a positive plan of action. In Egan's step IIA he refers to 'developing a preferred scenario'. Egan considers that goal setting is the point when clients are encouraged to move from 'a reactive symptomatic position to a pro-active concern and planning for a healthier life and sense of well being'. In emphasising the power and benefits of goal setting, Egan (1995) stresses that helping clients to identify goals mobilizes them into action and helps to focus attention and energy. He proposes that counsellors ask the following question: 'What do you have to do to get what you want?' Egan (1995) suggests asking clients to formulate future-oriented questions related to the current problem, based on the clients' 'wants' and 'needs'. Clients are requested to imagine what the situation might look like if it looked a little better and are then encouraged to write down a review of the possibilities.

Glasser (1989) proposes that human behaviour is engineered to achieve the fulfilment of human 'wants' and 'needs', and problematic behaviours are seen as the lingering unmet needs and wants which exist in the here and now. In establishing a structured positive plan of action (goals), Glasser also asks the questions 'What do you want?' and 'What do you *really* want?' When clients determine their 'really wants' they are uncovering the needs they wish to fulfil. Both Egan and Glasser talk of needs and wants in determining goals, but with a slightly different emphasis.

Different Goals

In a situation where the client and counsellor have different goals the most crucial position a counsellor can take is to be sincere, genuine and respectful of the client's ability to set his or her own goals. Periodically the client's and counsellor's goals may be different and in these instances it is generally believed that unless someone is at risk, the best way forward is to work with the client's goals (Velleman, 1992). For example, if a problem drinker wishes to adopt a controlled approach to drinking and the counsellor considers that abstinence might be a more appropriate goal, a suitable course of action might be for the counsellor to explore his/her reservations with the client and to explain why his/her goal might be different to that of the client, but at the same time to respect the client's desire for an alternative goal.

Domestic violence, usually the physical abuse of women by their male partners, is another area that might present a challenge, in that the counsellor's goals may differ from the client's. In cases where the client is at risk, safety is a primary consideration for the counsellor when helping the client to determine counselling goals. However, the client's goal may be to change the abusing partner's behaviour. The counsellor in this instance needs to be constantly aware of the client's safety while exploring the options, and at the same time to respect the client's autonomy.

Practice Points

Assess the client's real wants and needs.

Whilst being respectful of the client's wants and needs, it is important to demonstrate congruence.

Evaluation of Goal Achievement

It is generally accepted that goals should be measurable (Sutton, 1989). Noting how things are at an assessment session provides a baseline measure for future appraisal. It is important for both counsellor and client to be able to recognise and identify a measure of change. For example, when working with clients with alcohol problems the number of units of alcohol consumed will be noted at the initial session and used as a baseline measure in future sessions.

I carried out a research project in the alcohol field whereby clients were asked to self-evaluate how close they were to reaching their goals at the end of each session. This approach to goal-assessment was initially based on research by Sutton (1989). This model of evaluating counselling, the goal attainment approach, was used with some differences.

At the end of the assessment session and each subsequent session, the counsellors left the clients with a questionnaire to complete, requesting them to self-monitor how close they considered they were towards reaching their goals. For example:

How close are you towards reaching your goal?

very close	moderately close	neither close nor far	moderately far	very far
1	2	3	4	5

This scale of measurement is called a Likert scale. These scales are useful in that little time is involved in completing them and they are generally user-friendly.

In the initial assessment session the counsellor and client agreed a goal which utilized the above mentioned criteria. Such goals might include: 'I will be drinking 20 units of alcohol per week in six weeks' time.' Goals were written down as part of the counselling practice. It was agreed that this self-monitoring would be assessed and discussed at the review session (session 6).

Research (Stiles, 1980) indicates that four to six sessions give an adequately stable index and allow trends and relationships to be analysed.

It was considered important that clients did not feel inhibited by counsellors and that their desire to please the counsellors should not influence their self-monitoring. These concerns were behind the decision to leave the clients time alone to complete the questionnaire.

This approach differs from Sutton's 'goal attainment model' in that Sutton invited clients to indicate, on a scale from - 5 to + 5, how close they were towards reaching their agreed goal as a component part of the counselling session (see Chapter 8). Sutton considers that discussion of progress on a sessional basis can produce beneficial results in that progress towards goals can be reinforced and movement away from the agreed goal can be assessed.

As a component of my research I felt it was important not to have any influence on clients' self-monitoring, in an attempt to overcome experimenter effects. 'Experimenter effects' is a statistical term which refers to processes in a psychological experiment whereby the subjects, in attempting to please the experimenter, will respond to such cues as tone of voice, harshness or friendliness, sharpness of movement, and involuntary noises of pleasure or despair, which can all influence the client (in this case) to respond in a way that he or she might consider would please the counsellor.

This is not to say that goals were not discussed in the course of counselling. They were addressed in a more general sense. For example, in attempting to analyse a drinking binge, in the case of the client who is attempting to control his or her drinking the number of units consumed would be a significant factor.

Practice Points

In the assessment session, identify and make explicit problematic behaviour as a baseline measure for change.

Explain self-monitoring to clients.

Write goals down.

Case Example

A 24 year old single man living with his mother, Tim described himself as 'worthless' and his life as 'meaningless'. He came for advice and counselling regarding his alcohol intake, as he was experiencing many emotional, psychological and social problems associated with his drinking.

In attempting to estimate to what extent Tim's drinking was a problem, or was contributing to other problems, a number of factors were examined:

- his alcohol use
- his drinking patterns
- the effects of the use of alcohol
- his thinking concerning the alcohol use (expectations, values, definition of the problem, understanding its cause)
- the context (family, employment, social) within which he has been drinking.

Tim was drinking 70 units of alcohol per week. He was drinking daily, usually alone and secretively, which was a source of added concern for him. If he was drinking with 'mates' he considered it would not be quite so problematic.

Public health guidelines for sensible drinking in the UK are that regular consumption of two to three units a day by women of all ages constitutes a low level of risk. Consistently drinking three or more units a day is not advised. For men of all ages the regular consumption of three to four units a day constitutes a low level of risk. Consistently drinking four or more units a day is not advised. (However, it is worth noting that there is some disagreement over the sensible drinking limits in Britain.)

Tim's drinking began at age 18 and was linked to his inability to mix socially without alcohol. His drinking increased gradually from social to problematic drinking throughout the working day which was a contributory factor in his dismissal. At this time he was drinking upwards of 120 units of alcohol per week. Tim, who is now 25, had at no time been alcohol free in the intervening years; therefore, he had not experienced withdrawal symptoms.

An important responsibility at the initial assessment session is to provide clients with information, and in Tim's case he did not know how much alcohol was too much. Therefore, an essential part of the assessment was to provide him with the necessary information to make an informed decision about his drinking.

Tim considered that he wanted to adopt a controlled approach to drinking and felt a gradual reduction in alcohol consumption was the most appropriate course of action. He felt that a realistic goal for the first week might be a reduction of 20 units of alcohol from the current 70 units to 50 units. Most of Tim's drinking was done secretively and alone, so he felt that a secondary aim might be to go to the pub to drink socially. He agreed to self-monitor his goal progress over a six session period.

Intervention

The first session following the assessment involved examining Tim's drinking and addressing thoughts, anxieties, fears and beliefs around alcohol. He felt that alcohol provided him with the necessary 'guts' to be able to interact with people, but at the same time feared that he was portraying himself in a negative light: 'I am not a nice person when I have been drinking.' Overall his drinking and its effects resulted in him having a sense of self-loathing. Therefore, in terms of costs and benefits, alcohol consumption resulted in Tim feeling negative about himself, whilst at the same time enabling him to mix socially. At this stage we began to discuss the *choices* he had and the ways in which he could effect change in his life.

The general trend for the two subsequent sessions followed a similar pattern to the above: reviewing Tim's level of alcohol consumption; exploring alternative coping strategies; helping him to work out a plan of action, with contingency plans; and identifying ways in which he had dealt with situations constructively, which he might previously have found difficult. Facilitating and restraining forces were examined which might help or hinder Tim towards reaching his goal: support from others, money, craving, danger times, past successes and failures. Working with Tim centred on reducing restrainers and strengthening facilitators.

Tim's appearance gradually improved, and he presented as more positive and confident in the counselling sessions.

Session 4–6
The general content of these three sessions involved raising Tim's awareness of the internal forces that might have pushed him towards excessive and solitary drinking, and then using more active techniques to help him rethink his options in these circumstances.

Raising Awareness
Analysis of Tim's drinking episodes enabled him to get a better knowledge of how much alcohol he was actually consuming. It made him aware of the circumstances in which the activity occurred – what actually triggered off a drinking bout.

Other awareness techniques utilised were described by Wallace (1985), and include: 'following the drink through', which involves the client imagining vividly the entire drinking episode, concentrating on the more delayed negative consequences as well as the initial positive ones; and 'talking to yourself', in which the client has a conversation with him or herself, alternating between the sober and the drunk self, in order to 'sharpen and clarify the inner conflict commonly encountered'.

Restructuring Tim's Thinking about his Drinking Behaviour
The above techniques for raising awareness provided a basis upon which Tim could be helped to rethink his drinking behaviour. In

Tim's case this involved looking at the differences between the times in his life when he could drink socially and his current secretive drinking behaviour. Other strategies discussed with him included consciousness-raising and self-re-evaluation.

What all these techniques have in common is that they enable clients to think introspectively; to increase their awareness of their behaviour and motivation; to think about themselves in relation to their behaviour; and to question and re-evaluate this behaviour in the light of who they want to be and feel they can become.

This approach particularly appealed to Tim's logical way of thinking, whereby he could link his thought processes to subsequent actions. What he also appeared to find constructive was 'homework' between sessions; this involved practising relevant skills which offered an alternative way of coping with the triggers which normally pushed him into drinking.

There is a large amount of research relating to the issue of skills (summarised in Velleman, 1992), but in brief all the research backs up the finding that helping clients to acquire and practise skills as opposed to simply discussing the issue is of paramount importance.

Session 6: Review
Tim viewed himself more positively and no longer had feelings of self-loathing and worthlessness following the six weeks of counselling.

He reported that within the last two weeks he had begun to mix socially. He had enrolled on a City & Guilds computer course and his life was taking on new meaning and a sense of purpose. Analysis of Tim's goal achievement over the six session period indicated that he had decreased his alcohol consumption from 70 units to 30 units per week and he had monitored his goal progress in the following manner:

Week 1: assessment	very far
Week 2	moderately close
Week 3	neither far nor close
Week 4	neither far nor close
Week 5	moderately close
Week 6	moderately close

Working with Tim in this way helped him to learn to look at himself introspectively, and to replace the destructive picture of himself with another more positive one that did not depend on alcohol. During the time between sessions, Tim put into practice the various strategies that had evolved during the sessions. He became more skilled at seeing at-risk situations, avoiding them, and utilising his new-found abilities to deal with, rather than drink away, difficulties.

Tim's level of awareness about his drinking was increased by focusing on his goal at the end of each session. However, he lacked alternative ways of behaving and the skills to carry these out. The sessions ended with him being offered the opportunity to practise the skills he had learnt, but to return for further coun-selling in the future if he felt the need to do so.

This case example highlights how the issue of goal setting is addressed in each session in a non-judgemental way, allowing the client space to self-monitor at the end of each session, by highlighting for himself how close he considered he was towards reaching his goal.

Discussion
The case presented supports the concept that controlled drinking is an attainable goal for some clients. However, Tim was highly motivated and had clear and concise goals prior to attending the counselling sessions. Working with clients who hold ambiguous feelings regarding behaviour change may take longer to engage and the counselling contract in such cases would be renewed following each six week contract.

My work with Tim within a broadly cognitive-behavioural framework, with its clear emphasis on logical consequences of personal actions and the importance of personal control, seemed both appropriate and beneficial. He made excellent progress in terms of both behaviour change and personal growth. He was able to identify his wants and needs, to examine his behaviours, and to formulate better ways to achieve fulfilment and satisfaction. To this end the counselling was successful.

What Do Purchasers of Treatment Services Want from Evaluation?

Individuals who pay for their own counselling can judge for them-selves whether the counselling has been successful. Institutional purchasers, however, such as government agencies, employers, etc., are not in a position to make such judgement and need objective and verifiable evidence that goals have been achieved.

A list of client characteristics that may affect outcome has been identified by Longabaugh and Lewis (1988) and includes the following:

- client age
- client gender
- psychological variables including psychiatric diagnosis, psychological health indices, and level of client coping skills
- marital status
- client employment status
- socio-economic status
- environmental stressors and supports available.

When evaluating goal attainment in counselling, one or more of these factors may be related to successful outcome. For example, research might indicate in the alcohol field that clients who are married and employed are more likely to achieve a goal of controlled drinking than those who are unmarried and unemployed, for whom a more appropriate goal might be abstinence. The efficacy of financial and psychological input is highly correlated to counselling assessment of social status.

In many instances providers of counselling services limit the analysis of counselling effectiveness (goal attainment) to clients who complete the agreed number of counselling sessions. Although this is important knowledge, the consideration of attrition during counselling can provide critical information for both the providers and the purchasers of counselling services. On this basis outcome measures should represent not only those clients who achieve goals but also those who do not, and those who do not complete the agreed number of counselling sessions.

Practice Points

Be attentive to purchasers' needs.

Monitor number of counselling sessions.

Observe clients who do not achieve goals.

What Aspects of Clients' Functioning Before and After Counselling Should Be Measured?

Three indicators are commonly agreed to be important for an analysis of functioning and might be included in evaluation:

1   Personal well-being is important because people are likely to hope that they will feel better about themselves and their lives after counselling.
2   The client's performance in various life roles such as family member, friend, worker, etc. also has an impact on what might be considered effective outcome or goal achievement. A counselling goal in this instance might be 'to be able to communicate with my family'.
3   Knowledge of physical health status before and after counselling is essential in that clients may be experiencing physiological manifestations of psychological ill-health. In specific areas such as the drug and alcohol fields, physical health status prior to intervention is essential in that health improvement over time is associated positively with abstinence/control. The goal in this instance might be 'to feel better physically'.

The above mentioned functions are important considerations for both counsellors and providers in that they may be utilised as measures of outcome and incorporated into goal setting.

Practice Points

Assess clients' functioning.

Consider three indicators: personal well-being; performance in life roles; physical health.

Analysis

From the counsellor's and client's perspective, analysis involves evaluating the facilitating and restraining forces influencing whether or not the client is close to reaching their goal. At the review session, if a client is neither close nor far from reaching his/her goal, the analysis might involve identifying what facilitating factors helped the client to move from very far to

Table 6.1 *Example of client self-monitoring over six sessions*

Week	Very far	Moderately far	Neither close nor far	Moderately close	Very close
1	89%	9%	2%	0	0
2	57%	27%	16%	0	0
3	21%	24%	28%	27%	0
4	10%	12%	17%	20%	41%
5	5%	6%	11%	20%	58%
6	1%	3%	5%	18%	73%

moderately far and what restraining factors are inhibiting the client from moving from moderately far to moderately close.

In considering 'quality of care', the question that springs to mind is 'Did the patient get better?' This question is fundamental to the entire process of service provision. In the past both providers and funders lacked the means to collect data and purchasers effectively bought service efforts rather than results. This trend is rapidly changing and today's purchasers are seeking demonstrable results for both themselves and clients. It might reasonably be assumed that purchasers would consider a measurement of goal achievement as an indicator of service success.

The goal achievement model might therefore be utilised to highlight the percentage of clients who have reported how close they are to reaching their goals over a six week period. This involves analysing the mean percentage of clients who reported being very far from reaching their goals in sessions 1, 2, 3 and so on. This can most usefully be represented by means of a chart indicating what percentage of clients are very close to reaching their goal at the end of session 6: an example is given in Table 6.1. There is also adequate information available to further break this down to percentages for each session, for example what percentage of clients were at what stage of progress at week 3 and whether this relates to another factor such as age of client.

Practice Points

Become familiar with the Likert scale of measurement.

Practise basic statistical analysis, for example mean, medium, mode.

Conclusion

What Lieske (1986) has said of nursing applies also to counselling: 'a widespread responsibility on the part of all professional practitioners should be to make some contribution, in some way, to the validation of their practice'. Evaluation goal achievement could be viewed as beneficial to the verification of counselling practice as well as increasing practical knowledge and clinical skills. Generally speaking counselling is based on the principle of enabling clients to achieve their potential (goal) within the limitations of their capabilities and environment, and it could therefore be reasonably argued that evaluation of goal achievement in counselling is beneficial for client, counsellor and purchasers.

The focus of this chapter has been on the alcohol field, but the structured intervention and method of evaluation described can be utilised for clients presenting with various problems such as depression, anxiety and relationship difficulties. The above mentioned Likert scale can be employed and adapted as a tool for measuring psychological and emotional well-being. More importantly this is a client-led evaluation which is both empowering and non-intrusive.

I would like to stress that this is a very basic approach to evaluation. It might be considered by counsellors who are tentatively beginning to ask 'How do I measure counselling outcome?' Questions to consider might be 'What do purchasers want?' and furthermore 'What do clients want?'

References

Bordin, E.S. (1979) 'The generalisability of the psychoanalytic concept of the working alliance', *Psychotherapy: Theory, Research, and Practice*, 16: 252–9.

De Shazer, S. (1986) *Keys to Solution in Brief Therapy*. New York: W.W. Norton.

Dryden, W. (1989) *Key Issues for Counselling in Action*. London: Sage.

Egan, G. (1995) *The Skilled Helper: an Approach to Effective Helping* (4th edn). Brooks/Cole.

Glasser, N. (1989) *Control Theory in the Practice of Reality Therapy*. New York: Harper & Row.

Janis, I.L. and Mann, L. (1977) *Decision Making: a Psychological Analysis of Conflict, Choice, and Commitment*. New York: Free Press.

Lieske, A.M. (1986) *Clinical Nursing Research*. Rockville, MD: Aspen.

Longabaugh, R. and Lewis, D.C. (1988) 'Key issues in treatment outcome studies', *Alcohol, Health & Research World*, 12(3).

Maslow, A. (1954) *Motivation and Personality* (2nd edn). New York: Harper & Row.

Reber, A.S. (1985) *Dictionary of Psychology*. New York: Penguin.

Stiles, W.B. (1980) 'Measurement of the impact of psychotherapy sessions', *Journal of Counselling and Clinical Psychology*, 48, 176–85.

Sutton, C. (1989) 'The evaluation of counselling: a goal-attainment approach', in W. Dryden (ed.), *Key Issues for Counselling in Action*. London: Sage.

Velleman, R. (1992) 'Counselling people with alcohol and drug problems', in W. Dryden, D. Charles-Edwards and R. Woolfe (eds), *Handbook of Counselling in Britain*. London: Routledge.

Wallace, J. (1985) 'Behavioural modification methods as adjuncts to psychotherapy', in S. Limberg, J. Wallace and S. Blume, *Practical Approaches to Alcoholism Psychotherapy* (2nd edn). New York: Plenum.

7 *Modality Assessment*

Stephen Palmer

Arnold Lazarus (1981; 1989) believes that the entire range of human personality can be included within seven modalities. He places emphasis on the fact that people are essentially biological organisms (neurophysiological/biochemical entities) who behave (act and react), emote (experience affective responses), sense (respond to olfactory, tactile, gustatory, visual and auditory stimuli), imagine (conjure up sights, sounds and other events in the mind's eye), think (hold beliefs, opinions, attitudes and values), and interact with one another (tolerate, enjoy or endure various interpersonal relationships). By referring to these seven discrete but interactive dimensions or modalities as **b**ehaviour, **a**ffect, **s**ensation, **i**magery, **c**ognition, **i**nterpersonal and **d**rugs/ biology, the useful acronym **BASIC ID** arises from the first letter of each (see Palmer and Lazarus, 1995).

In this chapter I will look at the benefits of undertaking comprehensive modality assessments of clients, how to assess the seven modalities, and what to do once the assessment is completed. The modality assessment described is suitable for use in counselling, psychotherapy and stress management (Palmer, 1992).

Why Modality Assessments?

During the 1980s when I first began to train and supervise counsellors, therapists and stress management trainers I became aware that often helpers did not have a sound understanding of their clients' problems. This had an adverse effect upon their work with individual clients as they were unsure how to proceed or what strategies to adopt or interventions to make. In addition, this confusion would sometimes heighten their own anxiety levels. Their limited grasp of the overall picture would occasionally lead them to focus on the least useful issues in the session, for example, attempting to help a client overcome a particular phobia whilst ignoring her suicidal ideation and severe depression.

I realised it would be very useful for counsellors (and myself) to have a simple but comprehensive assessment procedure which would guide them through the client's maze of problems without overlooking any important aspect. On researching the subject of assessment I decided to take an in-depth look at Lazarus's multimodal assessment format and a multimodal framework. I discovered that the relatively simple procedures allowed inexperienced counsellors to gain great insight into a client and his or her particular problem(s). The trainee counsellors and supervisees started to really understand what it was like to step into their clients' shoes and take their view of the world. In my opinion, this holistic approach enhanced the quality of the counselling being offered and convinced me that clients were being short changed if they received anything less.

However, it is worth noting that not every client needs a full modality assessment and counselling programme across the entire BASIC ID: for example, a person suffering from a simple phobia may only require a couple of the key modalities analysed in depth. Also the counsellor needs to be aware of a client's temperament as some individuals may feel overwhelmed when asked too many questions or given numerous forms to complete. I would concur with Dryden and Feltham (1992: 71) who note that client temperament is 'an important area, often overlooked or not well understood by counsellors'.

Responses to Stress

Individuals who enter counselling will generally have a number of difficulties they wish to discuss and resolve. Clients seldom come to counselling if life is going well and they are feeling happy! If the counsellor wishes to undertake a full BASIC ID assessment, it is useful to know the typical responses to stress or difficult life events (past, present or anticipated) a client may experience. Table 7.1 places the responses to stress under headings which correspond to the BASIC ID framework. This will help in deciding

Table 7.1 *Responses to stress on BASIC ID modalities*

Behaviour
Avoidance/phobias
Alcohol/drug abuse
Insomnia/sleep disturbances
Increased caffeine/nicotine intake
Over-eating/loss of appetite
Restlessness
Anorexia/bulimia
Comfort eating
Poor driving
Accident proneness
Aggression/irritability
Poor time management
Low productivity
Increased absenteeism
Compulsive behaviour
Checking rituals
Impaired speech/voice tremor
Nervous cough
Impulsive behaviour
Tics, spasms
Withdrawing from relationships
Teeth grinding
Clenched fists
Type A behaviour, e.g. walking/talking/
    eating faster; hostile, competitive,
    heightened awareness of time
Sulking behaviour
Decreased/increased sexual activity
Frequent crying
Poor eye contact
Unkempt appearance

Affect
Anxiety
Anger
Depression
Guilt
Grief
Sadness
Hurt
Shame/embarrassment
Morbid jealousy
Suicidal feelings

Sensation
Headaches
Tension
Rapid heartbeat
Palpitations
Nausea
Aches/pains
Tremors/inner tremors
Indigestion
Butterflies in stomach
Spasms in stomach
Abdominal cramps
Feeling faint/dizziness
Vaginismus/psychogenic dysparenunia
Premature ejaculation/erectile dysfunction
Dry mouth
Cold sweat
Clammy hands
Numbness
Sensory flashbacks

Imagery (images of)
Losing control
Helplessness
Isolation/being alone
Becoming a bag lady/man (or tramp)
Failure
Accidents/injury
Shame/humiliation/embarrassment
Dejection, rejection
Physical/sexual/mental abuse
Self and/or others dying/suicide
Poor self-image
Nightmares/distressing recurring dreams
Visual flashbacks
Persistent daydreams

Cognition
'Life should not be unfair'
'I must perform well'
'I must be in control'
'It's terrible, awful, horrible, unbearable'
    etc.
'I must have what I want'

continued

Table 7.1   *(continued)*

'I/others must obey my moral code and rules'	Suspicious/secretive
'Others must approve of me'	Co-dependency
Cognitive distortions, e.g. all-or-nothing thinking, magnification, minimisation, etc.	Sex addiction
Self/other damning statements, e.g. idiot, stupid, bastard	*Drugs/biology*
'If I fail, this proves that I'm a total failure'	Diarrhoea/constipation/flatulence
Low tolerance to frustration statements, e.g. 'I can't stand it'	Use of drugs, stimulants, alcohol, tranquillisers, hallucinogens
	Allergies/skin rash
Interpersonal	Frequent urination
Timid/unassertive	Epilepsy/seizures
Passive/aggressive in relationships	Cancer
No friends	High blood pressure/coronary heart disease (angina/heart attack)
Loner	Dry skin
Avoidant	Chronic fatigue/exhaustion/burn-out/ rust-out
Withdrawn	Diabetes
Competitive	Asthma
Sycophantic behaviour	Frequent flu/common cold
Puts others' needs before one's own/ placatory	Rheumatoid arthritis
Makes friends easily/with difficulty	Lowered immune system (reduction in lymphocytes and eosinophils)
Manipulative tendencies	Sleep disturbances
Gossiping	Organic problems
	Poor nutrition, exercise and recreation
	Biologically based mental disorders

under what modality to place a particular problem in the assessment stage (see Palmer and Dryden, 1995).

The table of responses to stress should only be used as a rough guide, although it does give some indication of what to look for in each modality. It is worth noting that individuals who have been suffering from stress for a long time may eventually develop problems of a physical nature, such as hypertension, diabetes or serious heart disease. I have found that clients who undertake bibliotherapy by reading a guide (for example, Palmer and Strickland, 1995) about stress management, either before or soon after the first counselling session, are usually able to accurately report their specific stress-related problems. This generally gives the counsellor an early insight into the client's symptoms and subsequently a suitable counselling programme can be rapidly developed. We return to possible modality interventions later in this chapter.

The Modality Assessment Procedure

Many approaches to counselling are trimodal, focusing on affect, behaviour and cognition, and may overlook important areas such as the interpersonal and imagery modalities. Although all of the BASIC ID modalities may be considered by therapists adhering to these approaches, the counsellor may not always systematically address them, thereby overlooking vital information. This section will illustrate how the counsellor can ensure that no stone (or modality) is left unturned.

Assuming that the client does not arrive in a very distressed state, then a thorough assessment of the modalities can be undertaken. Some of the questions asked are shown in Table 7.2 (based on Lazarus, 1981; Lazarus and Lazarus, 1991; Palmer and Dryden, 1995).

The information in the table can be gradually obtained over a period of time. It is not essential to cover all of these points in the first interview. Depending upon the problem(s) the client presents, different modalities can be explored. Often clinically relevant information can be obtained from a thorough search of each modality. However, this can be time consuming. I have found that the 15 page Multimodal Life History Inventory (MLHI: Lazarus and Lazarus, 1991) can be used to derive the majority of the required details (see Appendix). If the client is asked to complete the questionnaire at home, then valuable therapeutic time can be saved. In my experience most clients are keen to help the counsellor understand their problems and are able to see the benefits of completing the MLHI. To ensure the client is willing to complete the MLHI, it is important to introduce it with care near the end of the first session. A typical dialogue is as follows:

> *Counsellor:* I believe that I've started to understand some of the issues involved with your problems. One of the main themes appears to be anxiety about social situations at work and in your personal life.
> *Client:* I have to agree with you. I've been anxious about social situations since I was a child.
> *Counsellor:* I have found it very useful if my clients complete this questionnaire at home. [*Counsellor shows client the MLHI.*] It saves me taking up a lot of your time here asking questions about

Table 7.2   *Client assessment questions on BASIC ID modalities*

Behaviour

What would you like to start or stop doing?

What behaviours are preventing you from being happy?

What do you avoid doing?

When do you procrastinate?

Are 'significant others' doing things you would like to do?

What is holding you back from doing things that you want to do?

What skills would you like to develop further?

How does your behaviour affect your relationships (or emotions, or images, or
    sensations, or thoughts, or health)?

Affect

What do you cry about?

What do you laugh about?

What do you get angry about?

What do you get anxious about?

What do you get depressed about?

What do you get sad about?

What do you get guilty about?

What do you get jealous about?

What do you get envious about?

What do you get hurt about?

Do you persistently have a recurring negative emotion?

How do your emotions affect your relationships (or behaviour, or images, or
    sensations, or thoughts, or health)?

Sensation

What do you like to taste?

What do you like to see?

What do you like to touch?

What do you like to hear?

What do you like to smell?

What do you dislike tasting?

What do you dislike seeing?

What do you dislike touching?

What do you dislike hearing?

What do you dislike smelling?

What unpleasant sensations do you suffer from, if any? (e.g. tremors, pains, tension,
    light-headedness, etc.)

How do you feel emotionally about any of your sensations? (e.g. do you become
    anxious about your tremors etc.?)

How do your sensations affect your relationships (or behaviour, or images, or thoughts,
    or health)?

University of Nottingham
School of Nursing &
Derbyshire Royal Infirmary
London Road
DERBY DE1 2QY

continued overleaf

Table 7.2   (continued)

Imagery

Can you describe your self-image (or body image)?

What images do you have that you like?

What images do you have that you dislike?

When you have these negative images, do you feel less or more anxious (or guilty, or depressed etc.)?

Can you describe any recurrent dreams or nightmares you may have?

Can you describe any recurrent daydreams you may have?

Can you describe any pleasant/unpleasant flashbacks (or memories) you may have?

Can you picture any scene that you find relaxing?

In moments of solitude, do you picture any particular event from your past or have any fantasy about the future?

What do you picture yourself doing in the immediate future?

What do you picture yourself doing in two years' (and/or five years', and/or ten years', and/or twenty years', and/or fifty years') time?

How do these images affect your emotions (or behaviour, or thoughts, or sensations, or relationships, or health)?

Cognition

What are your main musts, shoulds, oughts, have/got tos?

What are your main wants, wishes, desires and preferences?

What are your main values that you believe are important?

What are your beliefs that you believe are important?

In key areas of your life, what basic philosophy do you hold?

What perfectionist beliefs do you hold?

If you could use one word to describe yourself, what would it be?

If you could use one word to describe your main current problem, what would it be?

What are your major intellectual interests?

How do your thoughts affect your emotions (or behaviour, or sensations, or images, or relationships)?

Interpersonal

What expectations of others do you have?

What expectations do you think others have of you?

What expectations do you think society has of you?

How assertive (or aggressive, or passive) are you?

When are you most likely to be assertive (or aggressive, or passive)?

What people have been important in your life?

What people are important in your life?

How do the significant people in your life affect you (e.g. emotionally, practically etc.)?

Who has been the most significant person in your life?

How do you affect the significant people in your life?

continued

Table 7.2 *(continued)*

Who has said something to you that had/has a considerable effect on your outlook on life?

What social situations do you avoid (and/or prefer)?

To what extent are you either a loner or highly gregarious?

Drugs/biology

What are your main concerns about your health?

Have you ever undergone major surgery?

Are you on medication?

Do you take drugs?

Do you smoke? (If so, how many a day?)

Are you receiving adequate sleep?

Are you experiencing any sleeping difficulties?

How much alcohol do you drink in a week?

Can you describe your diet?

Have you tried to lose weight? (Were you successful?)

What type of exercise do you do?

Are you interested in improving your general health?

Do you believe that if you are taking regular exercise and eating a balanced diet, you will feel better about yourself?

Have significant others set you a good/poor health-related role model?

Source: based on Lazarus, 1981; Lazarus and Lazarus, 1991; Palmer and Dryden, 1995

different aspects of your life. It will not only focus on your anxiety, but may provide us with information that would help us to deal with your other problems too.

Client: It seems a good idea to me.

Counsellor: [*If any doubts are encountered in private practice the dialogue may continue.*] Incidentally, it saves your fees if you answer the questions in your own time as opposed to me asking them here in the session! Although it only takes about an hour, you don't have to complete the questionnaire in one sitting. You don't have to complete all the sections if you don't want to, and if you have any queries, we can look at them in the next session. Any questions?

Client: Seems straightforward.

Counsellor: [*Counsellor now highlights additional reasons for completing the MLHI by illustrating how modalities interact using a problem the client has previously mentioned.*] One section asks you about images and pictures you may have. The relevance of this section is that we find that most people who are unhappy or distressed tend to have negative images about their problems. For example, when you picture yourself going to a party do you have negative pictures in your mind's eye about what may happen?

Client: Yes I do.

Counsellor: When you visualise things going wrong, does this reduce
or increase your anxiety? [*Counsellor is demonstrating link between
imagery and affect modalities.*]

Client: It's funny you should ask that because when I picture things
going wrong, my anxiety goes through the roof.

Counsellor: This is exactly what we find with nearly all of our clients.
This information will really help us to deal with your problems. For
example, if we change the negative pictures then most of our clients
feel less anxious.

Although the previous dialogue illustrated how a counsellor might
introduce the MLHI to the client, it also showed the counsellor
highlighting the effect of two modalities upon each other. In
particular, clients are usually unaware of how the imagery modality
can influence how they feel about situations. If the client is not up
to completing the MLHI owing to inadequate skills or severe
depression, the counsellor can use the MLHI questions as a guide
in the session. However, if the counsellor decides not to use the
MLHI then key questions from Table 7.2 could be used. With
practice, the counsellor will be able to remember how to explore
each modality without referring to the list. Initially, to ensure that
each modality is explored, it is useful to start with behaviour and
proceed through the BASIC ID until each modality has been
assessed, keeping a note of the client's responses. Assessment can
be aided by audio-taping the session, which not only allows the
counsellor subsequently to listen carefully to the client's responses
but also provides a record which is useful for supervision purposes.

Practice Points

With very distressed clients, deal with the presenting problem first.
Return to a thorough modality assessment later.

Avoid overwhelming the client with too many questions. Remember to
build up a good therapeutic alliance.

Note whether particular modalities influence each other.

Demonstrate to clients how their behaviour, affect, sensations, imagery,
cognitions, interpersonal relationships and biological factors influence
their presenting problem(s).

Audio-taping of sessions may be beneficial for the client and aid
counsellor supervision. If audio-taping is used then ensure that the
client understands the benefits and explicitly gives permission for its use
in counsellor supervision.

> If a Multimodal Life History Inventory (MLHI) is used then give the client a clear rationale for its completion including the advantages to the client.
>
> Do not expect clients to complete the MLHI if they have deficits in writing skills or are severely depressed.

Modality Profile

Information obtained from the initial interview, and from a completed MLHI if used, helps the counsellor to construct a comprehensive modality profile (or BASIC ID chart) which consists of a modality analysis of the identified problems. Although this is not essential the modality profile can underpin the assessment and help to remind the counsellor of the different issues or problem areas in each modality. The modality profile serves as 'working hypotheses' which can be modified or revised as new information arises. The revision can form part of regular reviews. Table 7.3 shows John's modality profile. John had been referred by his doctor to the practice counsellor suffering from occupational stress. The Modality Profile indicated that John had high expectations of himself and others and this was a major contributory factor to his occupational stress (see Cognition).

The modality profile can be shared with the client to elicit comments and gain feedback, or can be used solely by the counsellor as a checklist or audit of key problem areas. Many adults are able to compile their own modality profile if they are given a typewritten instruction sheet (see box 1) describing each modality of the BASIC ID (adapted from Palmer and Dryden, 1995: 26–7). The names of some of the modalities have been altered to become more 'consumer-friendly'.

The client returns to the next session with his or her completed modality profile. Any difficulties or queries that arose in its completion are discussed and resolved with the counsellor. The problems recorded on the modality profile can become the specific areas that the client wishes to manage or resolve through counselling. This allows the counsellor and client to monitor progress and helps to keep both of them focused on the client's therapeutic goals.

Depending upon the therapeutic approach to counselling being used, counsellors may not wish to undertake a comprehensive

Table 7.3 *John's modality profile (or BASIC ID chart)*

Modality	Problem
Behaviour	Eats/walks fast, always in a rush, hostile, competitive: indicative of type A behaviour
	Avoidance of giving presentations
	Accident proneness
Affect	Anxious when giving presentations
	Guilt when work targets not achieved
	Frequent angry outbursts at work
Sensation	Tension in shoulders
	Palpitations
	Frequent headaches
	Sleeping difficulties
Imagery	Negative images of not performing well
	Images of losing control
	Poor self-image
Cognition	I must perform well otherwise it will be awful and I couldn't stand it
	I must be in control
	Significant others should recognise my work
	If I fail then I am a total failure
Interpersonal	Passive/aggressive in relationships
	Manipulative tendencies at work
	Always puts self first
	Few supportive friends
Drugs/biology	Feeling inexplicably tired
	Takes aspirins for headaches
	Consumes 10 cups of coffee a day
	Poor nutrition and little exercise

modality assessment during the usual course of therapy. For example, whereas multimodal therapists will normally construct a modality profile, person-centred and psychodynamic counsellors may not usually see much benefit in the exercise. However, when counsellors of any orientation find that their approach does not appear to be helping the client, then undertaking a modality profile may raise new areas for discussion during counselling. Blocks to change and improvement may be found, such as negative imagery or secondary gains from remaining phobic. Interactions between the modalities may be uncovered such as feeling anxious (affect) about becoming assertive (interpersonal) with the boss or partner.

A counsellor would need to give the client a rationale for undertaking a modality assessment at a later stage of counselling

Modality profile: client compilation instructions

Behaviours
This refers mainly to overt behaviours such as acts, gestures, habits, responses and reactions that can be observed. Write down which behaviours you would like to increase and which ones you would like to decrease. What would you like to stop doing? What would you like to start doing?

Feelings
This refers to emotions, moods and strong feelings. What emotions do you experience most often? Write down your unwanted emotions (e.g. anxiety, anger, depression, embarrassment, shame, guilt, hurt). Note under 'Behaviours' what you tend to do when you feel a certain way (e.g. avoid friends when depressed).

Physical sensations
Seeing, hearing, tasting, touching and smelling are our five basic senses. Make a list of any negative sensations that apply to you (e.g. butterflies in the stomach, blushing, dizziness, tension, pain, sweating). If any of these sensations cause you to act or feel in certain ways, ensure you note them down under 'Behaviours' or 'Feelings'.

Images
Write down any recurring dreams and any vivid memories that may be bothering you. Include any negative features about the way you see yourself (your self-image). We are looking for 'pictures' or vivid scenes from your past, present or future, that may be troubling you. If your images arouse any significant actions, feelings, or sensations, ensure that these items are added to 'Behaviours', 'Feelings', and 'Physical sensations'.

Thoughts
What sorts of ideas, opinions, values and attitudes get in the way of your happiness? Make a list of unhelpful things you tell yourself (e.g. 'I must be perfect at all times', 'I'm worthless and useless', 'I can't stand it', 'What's the point of living?'). What are some of your most irrational ideas? We are also interested in auditory memories that you keep on hearing and that constitute a problem (e.g. sad music). Note down how these thoughts and ideas influence your 'Behaviours', 'Feelings', 'Physical sensations' and 'Images'.

Interpersonal relationships
Write down any problems with other people (e.g. relatives, friends, work colleagues, neighbours, lovers, acquaintances) that bother you. Any concerns you have about the way other people treat you or how you treat them can appear here. Check through the items under 'Behaviours', 'Feelings', 'Physical sensations', 'Images' and 'Thoughts', and try to determine how they influence, and are influenced by, your 'Interpersonal relationships'.

Biological factors
Make a list of all drugs, whether prescribed by a doctor or not, that you are taking. Include any health and medical concerns, and major illnesses you have or have had. Write down whether you want to improve your diet, lose or gain weight, or take more exercise.

and this may depend upon the theory underpinning their approach. A typical dialogue is below:

Counsellor: We appear to have reached an impasse recently?
Client: You're right! I've reached a plateau and my problems don't seem to be improving any more.
Counsellor: I wonder whether we have overlooked some important issue. What do you think?
Client: I suppose that it is possible, but after three months of therapy, somewhat unlikely!
Counsellor: I'm not so sure. On some occasions I've found that if I spend one or two sessions focusing on reassessing the client's problems, looking at seven key areas of their personality, we can make useful gains. I examine their behaviour, that is what they actually do or avoid; emotions, that is how they feel about their problems; sensations, in other words, how they physically feel; mental images, for example, negative pictures they may regularly visualise; their thoughts, whether they are self-helping or self-defeating; their interpersonal relationships; and finally biological factors such as exercise, nutrition and other health-related issues like smoking or alcohol consumption. Often we find that some of these seven key areas interact and prevent the person from getting and staying better. A good example is when a person is physically unhealthy, overweight and drinks too much alcohol. This type of person may not have enough energy to deal with their current problems, whether it is panic attacks or a difficult relationship. Does this make sense to you?
Client: It seems to.
Counsellor: Would you like us to spend the rest of today's session closely examining these different areas?
Client: Okay. Let's start.

When a modality profile is developed after an impasse has been reached it is sometimes known as a second-order modality profile (or second-order BASIC ID). Generally second-order modality profiles solely focus on different aspects of a particular resistant problem (Lazarus, 1986). For example, Lazarus (1992) refers to a case where a male client did not respond to assertiveness training. His second-order modality profile indicated that he did not believe he was entitled to certain rights and privileges.

Palmer and Dryden (1995: 29) illustrated how a client had unsuccessfully used a relaxation exercise to reduce muscle tension. A second-order modality profile was undertaken which highlighted a number of important factors (see Table 7.4). It

Table 7.4 *Jack's second-order modality profile focusing on muscle tension*

Modality	Problem
Behaviour	'Hard-driving' behaviour, e.g. drives car fast, walks/eats fast, always in a rush (type A behaviour)
Affect	Easily angered
Sensation	Physically tense, especially at work, but not at weekends
Imagery	Images of getting angry with staff
Cognition	Thought muscle tension indicative of serious illness
	Awful to have a serious illness; staff must perform well; lack of self-acceptance
Interpersonal	Passive-aggressive with staff
	Withdraws from supportive relationships
Drugs/biology	Hypertension

appeared that the client, Jack, had a number of different problems that may have led to muscle tension. Jack's hard-driving, hostile, hurry-up approach to life (sometimes known as type A behaviour) led to interpersonal difficulties and little time to unwind and relax. In addition, on analysis, when he drove his car he tended to be hunched over his steering wheel. Jack's imagery triggered anger even before any staff difficulties arose. Assessment of the cognitive modality found that Jack thought muscle tension was indicative of a serious illness. This led to him concentrating on his physical symptoms whenever he did the relaxation exercise. This did not help him to relax.

In the last section of this chapter I will consider how a counsellor can move from modality assessment to formulating a counselling programme. In Jack's case, the counsellor discussed the benefits of 'slowing down' and driving in a more relaxed manner; used cognitive restructuring, information giving, and rational disputation to challenge his negative thoughts; provided coping imagery to help him stay calm; and offered assertion skills training to reduce passive-aggressive behaviour.

Practice Points

Avoid jargon. Use consumer-friendly language.

Share modality profiles with clients if you believe it will enhance therapeutic gains or improve the therapeutic alliance.

> Modality profiles are working hypotheses. Be prepared to modify or revise them in the light of new information or feedback from the client.
>
> Use modality profiles to monitor therapeutic progress.
>
> Use second-order modality profiles to examine blocks to change or resistant problems. Avoid viewing the client as 'resistant'.
>
> Discuss any difficulties or queries that the client may raise after completing an MLHI (if used).

Further Modality Assessment

Once a modality profile has been developed, specific problems may need further in-depth assessment. One of the most usual areas to assess is in the behaviour modality when a client is anxious about a range of different situations which he or she avoids. Research would suggest that a behavioural exposure programme is the most appropriate intervention in these cases. However, as the majority of clients would not necessarily agree to face their most anxiety triggering situation, a graded exposure programme is usually implemented. To undertake this task a ranked hierarchy of fears is constructed. The client is asked to rate their fears by using an arbitrary scale, such as from 0 to 10, where 0 represents no anxiety and 10 represents high anxiety or panic. Table 7.5 illustrates Margaret's hierarchy of fears (Palmer and Dryden, 1995: 94). She suffered from anxiety and panic attacks when travelling on public transport. Margaret first confronted the fear she believed she could tolerate. As she felt confident that the breathing exercise I had taught her would help to control her anxiety, she was willing to travel in a taxi unaccompanied. To monitor and assess her progress, she completed a homework diary after each graded exposure (Palmer and Dryden, 1995: 242; see Figure 7.1).

Similar to the behaviour modality, it may be necessary to construct a hierarchy of fears for an imaginal exposure programme. This is often used when *in vivo* or real-life exposure is difficult to arrange. For example, if Margaret had been too anxious to undertake the behavioural exposure programme, I would have started with an imaginal exposure programme to reduce her anxiety to within tolerable levels. Table 7.6 illustrates a typical hierarchy of fears for a person who is flying phobic (Palmer and Dryden, 1995: 83).

Table 7.5 *Hierarchy of fears for Margaret's behavioural exposure programme*

Rank	Subjective units of distress	Event
1	10.0	Standing in a crowded underground train that has stopped in a tunnel for longer than 10 minutes
2	9.5	Standing in a crowded underground train that has stopped in a tunnel for less than 10 minutes
3	9.0	Sitting in a crowded underground train that has stopped in a tunnel for longer than 15 minutes
4	8.5	Sitting in a crowded underground train that has stopped in a tunnel for less than 15 minutes
5	8.0	Standing in a crowded train or underground train during the rush hour
6	7.5	Sitting in a crowded train or underground train during the rush hour
7	7.0	Travelling a long journey on a crowded bus
8	6.5	Travelling a short journey on a crowded bus
9	6.0	Travelling on an uncrowded underground train
10	5.0	Travelling on an uncrowded train
11	4.5	Travelling on an uncrowded bus
12	4.0	Travelling in a taxi unaccompanied
13	3.0	Travelling in a taxi with a friend

Source: Palmer and Dryden, 1995: 94

The interpersonal modality assessment may indicate that assertion training would benefit a client. As in the previous examples, a ranked hierarchy of problem situations can be constructed as illustrated in Table 7.7. In this case, Marie, who worked in a training centre, was particularly concerned about her relationships with students and callers. However, do note that she decided to add non-work issues to the list as she found complaining on her own behalf very difficult. (see Figure 7.2 for a blank form.)

The client is asked which problem she would like to attempt first. It is advisable to start on one of the least difficult problems in the early stages of assertiveness training in order to build up the client's confidence. In Marie's case she decided to focus on being 'too obliging with her work colleagues'. To help me monitor her progress she completed an assertiveness behaviour diary after each exercise, which we later reviewed during the next therapy session (Palmer and Dryden, 1995: 245; see Figure 7.3).

Week commencing:

Name:

Therapist:

Goals for the week

1
2
3

| Date | Session | | Goal no. | Task performed | Anxiety | | | Comments |
	Began	Ended			Before	During	After	

0	2.5	5	7.5	10
No anxiety	Slight anxiety	Moderate anxiety	Marked anxiety	High anxiety/ panic

Figure 7.1 *Homework diary for exposure programme (Palmer and Dryden, 1995: 242)*

Table 7.6 *Hierarchy of fears for imaginal exposure programme*

Rank	Subjective units of distress	Event
1	10.0	Aeroplane crashing
2	9.5	Aeroplane taking off
3	9.0	Aeroplane landing
4	8.0	Aeroplane in turbulence
5	7.0	Imagining self becoming ill on the aeroplane
6	6.0	Aeroplane cruising
7	5.5	Aeroplane taxiing
8	5.0	Looking at aeroplane
9	4.5	Waiting for delayed plane in departure lounge
10	4.0	Waiting for plane in departure lounge
11	3.5	Parking the car in the airport car park
12	2.5	Driving to the airport
13	2.0	Reading brochure about holidays abroad

Source: Palmer and Dryden, 1995: 83

Table 7.7 *Assertiveness problem hierarchy form*

Name: Marie

Date: 27 June 1996

1   Difficulty in complaining with any services, e.g. motor trade

2   Dealing with situations where I feel vulnerable

3   Feeling unnecessarily guilty if I upset friends and family

4   Dealing with demanding students

5   Dealing with patronising callers on the telephone

6   Saying 'no' to my children

7   Being too obliging with friends

8   Being too obliging with work colleagues

9

10

11

12

Continue if necessary.

Name:

Date:

1 _____

2 _____

3 _____

4 _____

5 _____

6 _____

7 _____

8 _____

9 _____

10 _____

11 _____

12 _____

Continue if necessary.

Figure 7.2 *Assertiveness problem hierarchy form (Palmer and Dryden, 1995: 244)*

In the Drugs/biology Modality often it is useful to ask the client to monitor his or her alcohol consumption. One of the most straightforward ways a client can do this is by completing a Drinking Diary on a daily basis (see Figure 7.4). The Drinking Diary is later reviewed during the next therapy session.

Qualified psychologists and therapists who are registered to use psychological tests may find various inventories helpful when assessing and monitoring emotions in the Affect Modality. For example, the State-Trait Anger Expression Inventory (Spielberger, 1988), the Beck Depression Inventory (Beck and Steer, 1987), the Hopelessness Scale (Beck et al., 1974), the Maslach Burnout Inventory (Maslach and Jackson, 1986) and the State-Trait Anxiety Inventory (Spielberger et al., 1983).

Name:

Date	Situation	Person/people involved	Assertiveness skills used	Evaluation of skills	Areas for improvement

Figure 7.3 *Assertiveness behaviour diary (Palmer and Dryden, 1995: 245)*

Structural Profile

To obtain more information and also general goals for counselling, a structural profile can be drawn (Lazarus, 1989). This can be obtained by asking the client to rate subjectively, on a scale from 1 to 7, how she or he perceives her/himself in relation to the seven modalities. The counsellor can ask questions that focus specifically on each modality (adapted from Lazarus and Lazarus, 1991):

- *Behaviour* How much of a doer are you?
- *Affect* How emotional are you?
- *Sensation* How 'tuned in' are you to your bodily sensations?
- *Imagery* How much are you into mental images or pictures?
- *Cognition* How much of a 'thinker' are you?
- *Interpersonal* How much of a 'social being' are you?
- *Drugs/biology* To what extent are you health conscious?

If the MLHI is used, a section is devoted to eliciting this information, which saves therapeutic time. Once the scores from 1 to 7 are obtained for each modality, the counsellor can illustrate these scores graphically by representing them in the form of a bar chart

Day	What was consumed	When/where/with whom	Units	Total

Weekly total _____

Units (u): a rough guide

Ordinary strength beer, lager, cider:	half pint = 1 u; one pint = 2 u
Strong beer, lager, cider:	half pint = 2 u; one pint = 4 u
Wine (11% alcohol content):	standard glass = 1 u
Spirits:	standard English measure = 1 u
Sherry:	standard small measure = 1 u

Figure 7.4 *Drinking diary (Palmer and Dryden, 1995: 161)*

on graph or plain paper. Figure 7.5 shows Kate's structural profile. It can be seen that Kate perceives herself as a 'thinker' and a 'doer', as she rated herself at 7 on both the cognitive and behaviour modalities. On further investigation it transpired that her low inter-personal score of 2 was due to her perceiving herself as a 'loner'.

Once the structural profile has been discussed with the client, then a 'desired' structural profile can be contemplated. The client is asked in what way she would like to modify her profile during the course of therapy:

Counsellor: Kate, now you have seen your profile [*counsellor pointing to the profile*] it may be a good idea to consider each of the seven areas again and decide whether you would like to change them during the course of therapy. What do you think?

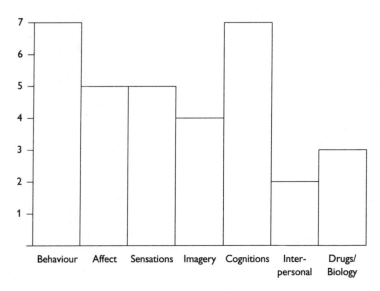

Figure 7.5 *Kate's structural profile*

Kate: Yeah. Sounds good.

Counsellor: Let's start at the biological factors. You have rated yourself at 3. Is this an area for change?

Kate: You bet. I really want to start taking regular exercise and stop smoking. In fact I know I should eat more fruit too!

Counsellor: What would be your desired score? [*Counsellor points to the 3 on the structural profile bar chart.*]

Kate: I reckon I could achieve 6. I reckon 7 will be unrealistic.

Counsellor: Can we make this more specific. You would like to stop smoking. Correct?

Kate: Yes.

Counsellor: What exercise do you want to do and how often?

Kate: I want to work out at the gym three times a week. My flatmate is already going. I can join her.

Counsellor: You mentioned fruit. What about us looking at your diet and seeing how it could be improved? I've got a number of guides and leaflets on this subject that may help.

Kate: Sounds fine.

This process is repeated for each modality and the new desired scores are transferred to a desired structural profile (see Figure 7.6). The counsellor ensures that a record of each specific target

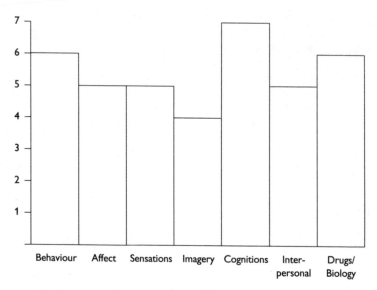

Figure 7.6 *Kate's desired structural profile*

or goal is kept. If there is sufficient room then each goal is written directly onto the profile, or if not it is kept in note form. The client is given a copy for his or her own records and as a reminder of what he or she would like to achieve during counselling. This helps to keep clients working towards their goals.

In many cases clients are keen to improve their drugs/biology modality as they believe that if they are physically feeling fine then they will feel emotionally better and more able to deal with other problems. However, the other modality scores do not necessarily reflect an area that needs change if they are either low or high. For example, a client may be happy being a 'doer' and having a subjective score of 7, whilst another client may decide that a score of 7 indicates that she is 'doing' too much or 'doing' too much of the wrong tasks and she would prefer a score of 5. In Kate's case, in discussion with her counsellor, she soon realised that being a loner (interpersonal score of 2) did not help her deal with occupational stress as she avoided seeking social support when facing major workplace problems. She decided that this would be a good area for improvement. Yet many other clients are happy to keep a low interpersonal score. It is important to remember that these are subjective scores that can help the counselling process and are usually unique to each client, especially in relation to the desired goals.

If the counsellor has contracted with the client to regularly review her or his counselling, then comparing the actual structural profile and the desired structural profile can form part of that review. When reviewing their counselling, clients will often want to revise their desired structural profiles. Often they realise that their goals or targets were set low, and as they achieve success in specific areas, with increased confidence, they then want to deal with more difficult issues such as being assertive with their manager or losing weight.

Counsellors who undertake couples or marital counselling have also found that using structural profiles can provide valuable information (Lazarus, 1989). In addition, the profiles can be compared in the session and used to highlight difficulties that a couple may be experiencing. For example, if one partner has a low interpersonal rating, while the other partner has a high rating, their interpersonal needs may be in direct conflict. The low scorer may wish to avoid social events while the high scorer may be extremely keen to socialise with family and friends. This can lead to bitterness with both parties. The counsellor can compare and contrast the different profiles and discuss them with both partners (see Palmer and Dryden, 1995). Counsellors may find that the Marital Satisfaction Questionnaire (see Figure 7.7) may also help them to assess clients in couples counselling.

Practice Points

After discussing each modality with the client, graphically illustrate structural profiles in the form of a bar chart, and share with the client.

Note specific desired goals. Avoid vague goals or targets.

Regularly review profiles with the client and revise goals if necessary.

Formulating a Counselling Programme

This book focuses on client assessment. However, this section will briefly show how modality profiles can be used to move from the assessment stage to the treatment stage. Otherwise modality

10	9	8	7	6	5	4	3	2	1	0

Pleased   Half yes   Not pleased
                                           Half no

After each question, write down the number that most closely approximates your present feelings about your marriage or your spouse.

I am:

1 Pleased with the amount we talk to each other.
2 Happy with the friends we share in common.
3 Satisfied with our sex life.
4 In agreement with the amount of time you or we spend at work and at home.
5 In agreement with the way we are spending money.
6 Pleased with the kind of parent you are. (If you have no children, are you pleased with your mutual plans for having, or not having, children?)
7 Of the opinion that you are 'on my team'.
8 Pleased with our leisure time together (e.g. sports, vacations, outings, etc.).
9 Basically in agreement with your outlook on life (e.g. values, attitudes, religious beliefs, politics, etc.).
10 Generally pleased with the way you relate to members of your own family (parents, siblings, etc.).
11 Satisfied with the way you relate to members of my family (e.g. my parents, siblings, etc.).
12 Pleased with your general habits, mannerisms, and overall appearance.

Add up your scores.

A total of 84 and more means that you have a *very good* marriage
Between 72 and 83 reflects *satisfactory* to *good* feelings and interactions
Below 60 indicates a *poor* level of marital satisfaction.

Figure 7.7 *Marital satisfaction questionnaire (Lazarus, 1989. Reprinted by permission of the Johns Hopkins University Press)*

assessment can increase the counsellor's understanding of a client and his or her problems, but the counsellor may not be sure of where to start and how to proceed.

Table 7.3 was John's modality profile, which highlighted the problems he was experiencing. In discussion and negotiation with John, this profile was modified to include possible therapeutic interventions. The revised profile (see Table 7.8) became the template for the counselling programme, keeping both John and the counsellor problem-focused. Careful analysis of the full

Table 7.8 *John's full modality profile (or BASIC ID chart)*

Modality	Problem	Proposed programme/treatment
Behaviour	Eats/walks fast, always in a rush, hostile, competitive: indicative of type A behaviour	Discuss advantages of slowing down; disadvantages of rushing and being hostile; teach relaxation exercise; dispute self-defeating beliefs
	Avoidance of giving presentations	Exposure programme; teach necessary skills; dispute self-defeating beliefs
	Accident proneness	Discuss advantages of slowing down
Affect	Anxious when giving presentations	Anxiety management
	Guilt when work targets not achieved	Dispute self-defeating thinking
	Frequent angry outbursts at work	Anger management; dispute irrational beliefs
Sensation	Tension in shoulders	Self-massage; muscle relaxation exercise
	Palpitations	Anxiety management e.g. breathing relaxation technique, dispute catastrophic thinking
	Frequent headaches	Relaxation exercise and bio-feedback
	Sleeping difficulties	Relaxation or self-hypnosis tape for bedtime use; behavioural retraining; possibly reduce caffeine intake
Imagery	Negative images of not performing well	Coping imagery focusing on giving adequate presentations
	Images of losing control	Coping imagery of dealing with difficult work situations and with presentations; 'step-up' imagery (Palmer and Dryden, 1995)
	Poor self-image	Positive imagery (Lazarus, 1984)
Cognition	I must perform well otherwise it will be awful and I couldn't stand it	Dispute self-defeating and irrational beliefs; coping statements; cognitive restructuring; ABCDE paradigm (Ellis et al., 1997); bibliotherapy; coping imagery (Palmer and Dryden, 1995)
	I must be in control	
	Significant others should recognise my work	
	If I fail then I am a total failure	

continued overleaf

Table 7.8   *(continued)*

Modality	Problem	Proposed programme/treatment
Interpersonal	Passive/aggressive in relationships	Assertiveness training
	Manipulative tendencies at work	Discuss pros and cons of behaviour
	Always puts self first	Discuss pros and cons of behaviour
	Few supportive friends	Friendship training (Palmer and Dryden, 1995)
Drugs/biology	Feeling inexplicably tired	Improve sleeping and reassess; refer to GP
	Taking aspirins for headaches	Refer to GP; relaxation exercises
	Consumes 10 cups of coffee a day	Discuss benefits of reducing caffeine intake
	Poor nutrition and little exercise	Nutrition and exercise programme

modality profile indicated that teaching John a suitable relaxation technique would help him deal or cope with a number of different problems. Daily use of a relaxation tape was chosen by John as the preferred intervention, whilst in the session the counsellor focused on helping John to dispute his self-defeating thinking and irrational beliefs. John's daily progress with his relaxation exercise was monitored by him completing a relaxation diary (Palmer, 1993: 52; see Figure 7.8). In addition John found coping imagery very beneficial.

It is worth noting that John's structural profile (SP) had scores of 7 in sensation and cognitive modalities. When high SP scores occur in a particular modality, often the person is responsive to techniques used from that modality. John found that the sensation and cognitive techniques were very helpful. This knowledge may aid the counsellor in technique selection (Lazarus, 1989; Mackay and Liddell, 1986; Michelson, 1986; Palmer and Dryden, 1995). A person may be referred to as a 'reactor' to a certain modality. Therefore John was a 'sensory reactor' and a 'cognitive reactor'. Likewise a person responsive to imagery is known as an 'imagery reactor'. Others include 'behavioural reactors' and 'physiological reactors'. This knowledge helps counsellors to be 'in tune' with their clients.

| Date | Session | | Time in minutes | Relaxation technique used | Tension levels Relaxed 0 Tense 10 | | Feelings | | Comments |
	Began	Ended			Before	After	During	After	
									Name:

Instructions: note the date, time, duration and type of relaxation exercise used. On a scale of 0–10, where 0 represents a relaxed state and 10 represents a tense state, write down scores before and after a training exercise. Monitor emotions and bodily feelings in the appropriate column. Record any variations to the technique used and any other comments.

Figure 7.8 *Relaxation diary (Palmer, 1993: 52. Reproduced with kind permission of The Centre for Multimodal Therapy)*

Table 7.9 *Frequently used techniques in multimodal therapy and training*

Modality	Therapy or training	Modality	Therapy or training

Behaviour	Behaviour rehearsal
	Empty chair
	Exposure programme
	Fixed role therapy
	Modelling
	Paradoxical intention
	Psychodrama
	Reinforcement
	  programmes
	Response prevention/cost
	Risk-taking exercises
	Self-monitoring and
	  recording
	Stimulus control
	Shame attacking
		Cognition	Bibliotherapy
			Challenging faulty
			  inferences
			Cognitive rehearsal
			Coping statements
			Correcting misconceptions
			Disputing irrational beliefs
			Focusing
			Positive self-statements
			Problem-solving training
			Rational proselytising
			Self-acceptance training
			Thought stopping

Affect	Anger expression
	Anxiety/Anger
	  management
	Feeling identification
		Interpersonal	Assertiveness training
			Communication training
			Contracting
			Fixed role therapy
			Friendship/intimacy
			  training

Sensation	Bio-feedback Hypnosis Meditation Relaxation training Sensate focus training Threshold training		Graded sexual approaches Paradoxical intentions Role play Social skills training

Imagery	Anti-future-shock imagery
	Associated imagery
	Aversive imagery
	Coping imagery
	Implosion and imaginal
	  exposure
	Positive imagery
	Rational emotive imagery
	Time projection imagery
		Drugs/biology	Alcohol reduction
			  programme
			Lifestyle changes, e.g.
			  exercise, nutrition, etc.
			Referral to physicians or
			  other specialists
			Stop smoking programme
			Weight reduction and
			  maintenance
			  programme

Source: adapted from Palmer, 1996: 55–6

As a number of techniques or interventions could be used for a particular problem (Palmer and Dryden, 1991; 1995), it is important to discuss the options with the client and allow the client to be actively involved in choosing the technique. Research has

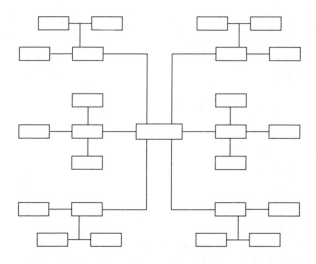

A stress map is a visual means of representing the sources of stress in your life. The central box represents yourself and the other boxes represent people you are in contact with. The other boxes can represent other potential stressors too, such as new computers or internal demands you place on yourself, e.g. perfectionist beliefs.

Complete the boxes and then rate the amount of stress each other potential stressor can cause you on a scale of 1 to 10, where 10 represents high levels of stress. Place the score next to the appropriate stressor. Then ask yourself how much stress you may cause the other people on your stress map. Also note these scores down.

Once the exercise is completed, note down any insights that you may have gained from undertaking stress mapping.

Figure 7.9 *Stress mapping (Palmer, 1990)*

highlighted the advantages of taking this approach. Lazarus (1973) demonstrated that if clients have a strong belief in the efficacy of a technique such as hypnosis then it is more likely to help them. This has been confirmed by a number of practitioners (for example, Palmer, 1993). Table 7.9 illustrates a number of key techniques used by multimodal and cognitive-behavioural therapists (Palmer, 1996).

There are many useful books on cognitive-behavioural techniques and strategies that can be utilised in developing a full modality profile (for example, Ellis, 1995; Ellis et al., 1997; Lazarus, 1984; 1989; Palmer and Dryden, 1995; McMullin, 1986; Scott et al.,

1995). Another technique to help the counsellor and client construct an overall picture of a specific problem or a range of problems is stress mapping (Palmer, 1990; see Figure 7.9). Non-cognitive-behavioural approaches to counselling, such as psychodynamic, person-centred and others too numerous to mention, may use different techniques, strategies or processes which could also be included on the full modality profile (for example, Barrett-Lennard, 1981; Dryden, 1989; Dunnett, 1988; Flegenheimer, 1982; Gendlin, 1981; Jacobs, 1988; Luborsky, 1993; Mann, 1982; Tomm, 1984).

Bayne (1993; 1995: 95) suggests that counsellors could use the Myers-Briggs Type Indicator (MBTI) to help in deciding 'which kinds of strategy are most and least likely to be effective with which clients'. The MBTI is based on some of Jung's ideas about personality and it measures four characteristics which are arranged in pairs of opposites: extroversion and introversion, sensing and intuition, thinking and feeling, and judging and perceiving. Similar to Lazarus's (1993) concept of the 'authentic chameleon', the counsellor can endeavour to adapt his or her counselling approach to one that will be most effective for the client. For example, Bayne (1995: 100) suggests that 'an extrovert counsellor with an introvert client' could deliberately talk less than usual. Counsellors can learn to adapt or match their approach even before they undertake a modality profile as they observe their clients in the initial counselling session.

Counsellors may need to adapt the framework illustrated in this chapter to their own particular approach. There are no hard and fast rules and the only limiting factors may be a counsellor's flexibility and creativity.

Practice Points

Actively engage the client in developing their counselling programme. Listen to their comments, opinions and concerns. Remember that it is their therapy, not yours!

Use the full modality profile as a flexible template for the counselling programme.

Carefully analyse the full modality profile and notice if any particular technique or intervention frequently appears. If it does then consider using the technique in the early stages of counselling unless this would be contra-indicated or could negatively affect the therapeutic alliance.

Look at the structural profile. If the client is a 'reactor' then seriously consider using techniques and strategies from the particular modality concerned. For example, use imagery techniques with 'imagery reactors'.

If an impasse is reached, undertake a full second-order modality profile focusing on issues related to the specific problem.

Conclusion

Assessment of the seven modalities by using modality profiles, second-order modality profiles, structural profiles, and question-naires such as the MLHI, can all help counsellors to undertake a more systematic approach to client assessment and in the sub-sequent formulation of an individual counselling programme (Palmer, 1992). The use of second-order modality profiles can also be helpful in dealing with blocks to change or when an impasse has been reached. The continual scanning of each modality and its interaction with every other can enhance a counsellor's effectiveness and awareness of the client's main problems. This chapter has focused on a holistic approach to understanding the client. With practice, counsellors may find the BASIC ID framework a useful tool.

Author's note

In Britain the Multimodal Life History Inventory is available from Centre for Multimodal Therapy, 156 Westcombe Hill, London, SE3 7DH.

References

Barrett-Lennard, G.T. (1981) 'The empathy cycle: refinement of a nuclear concept', *Journal of Counseling Psychology*, 28: 91–100.

Bayne, R. (1993) 'Psychological type, conversations and counselling', in R. Bayne and P. Nicholson (eds), *Counselling and Psychology for Health Professionals*. London: Chapman and Hall.

Bayne, R. (1995) 'Psychological type and counselling', *British Journal of Guidance and Counselling*, 23 (1): 95–106.

Beck, A.T. and Steer, R.A. (1987) *Beck Depression Inventory Manual*. San Antonio: The Psychological Corporation.

Beck, A.T., Weissman, A., Lester, D. and Trexler, L. (1974) 'The measurement of pessimism: the Hopelessness Scale', *Journal of Consulting and Clinical Psychology*, 42: 861–5.

Dryden, W. (1989) *Key Issues for Counselling in Action*. London: Sage.

Dryden, W. and Feltham, C. (1992) *Brief Counselling*. Buckingham: Open University Press.

Dunnett, G. (1988) *Working with People: Clinical Uses of Personal Construct Psychology*. London: Routledge.

Ellis, A. (1995) *Better, Deeper, and More Enduring Brief Therapy: the Rational Emotive Behavior Approach*. New York: Brunner/Mazel.

Ellis, A., Gordon, J., Neenan, M. and Palmer, S. (1997) *Stress Counselling: a Rational Emotive Behaviour Approach*. London: Cassell.

Flegenheimer, W.V. (1982) *Techniques of Brief Psychotherapy*. London: Jason Aronson.

Gendlin, E.T. (1981) *Focusing*. New York: Bantam Books.

Jacobs, M. (1988) *Psychodynamic Counselling in Action*. London: Sage.

Lazarus, A.A. (1973) '"Hypnosis" as a facilitator in behavior therapy', *International Journal of Clinical and Experimental Hypnosis*, 21: 25–31.

Lazarus, A.A. (1981) *The Practice of Multimodal Therapy: Systematic, Comprehensive and Effective Psychotherapy*. New York: McGraw-Hill.

Lazarus, A.A. (1984) *In the Mind's Eye: the Power of Imagery for Personal Enrichment*. New York: Guilford Press.

Lazarus, A.A. (1986) 'Multimodal therapy', in J.C. Norcross (ed.), *Handbook of Eclectic Psychotherapy*. New York: Brunner/Mazel.

Lazarus, A.A. (1989) *The Practice of Multimodal Therapy: Systematic, Comprehensive and Effective Psychotherapy* (revised edn). Baltimore, MA: Johns Hopkins University Press.

Lazarus, A.A. (1992) 'Multimodal therapy: technical eclecticism with minimal integration', in J.C. Norcross and M.R. Goldfried (eds), *Handbook of Psychotherapy Integration*. New York: Basic Books.

Lazarus, A.A. (1993) 'Tailoring the therapeutic relationship, or being an authentic chameleon', *Psychotherapy*, 30: 404–7.

Lazarus, A.A. and Lazarus, C.N. (1991) *Multimodal Life History Inventory*. Champaign, IL: Research Press.

Luborsky, L. (1993) 'How to maximise the curative factors in dynamic psychotherapy', in N.E. Miller et al. (eds), *Psychodynamic Treatment Research*. New York: Basic Books.

Mackay, W. and Liddell, A. (1986) 'An investigation into the matching of specific agoraphobic anxiety response characteristics with specific types of treatment', *Behaviour Research and Therapy*, 24: 361–4.

Mann, J. (1982) *A Casebook in Time-Limited Psychotherapy*. New York: McGraw-Hill.

Maslach, C. and Jackson, S.E. (1986) *Maslach Burnout Inventory: Second Edition*. Palo Alto, CA: Consulting Psychologists Press.

McMullin, R.E. (1986) *Handbook of Cognitive Therapy Techniques*. New York: Norton.

Michelson, L. (1986) 'Treatment consonance and response profiles in agoraphobia:

the role of individual differences in cognitive, behavioural and psychological treatments', *Behaviour Research and Therapy*, 24: 263–75.

Palmer, S. (1990) 'Stress mapping: a visual technique to aid counselling or training', *Employee Counselling Today*, 2 (2): 9–12.

Palmer, S. (1992) 'Multimodal assessment and therapy: a systematic, technically eclectic approach to counselling, psychotherapy and stress management', *Counselling*, 3 (4): 220–4.

Palmer, S. (1993) *Multimodal Techniques: Relaxation and Hypnosis*. London: Centre for Stress Management and Centre for Multimodal Therapy.

Palmer, S. (1996) 'The multimodal approach: theory, assessment, techniques and interventions', in S. Palmer and W. Dryden (eds), *Stress Management and Counselling: Theory, Practice, Research and Methodology*. London: Cassell.

Palmer, S. and Dryden, W. (1991) 'A multimodal approach to stress management', *Stress News*, 3 (1): 2–10.

Palmer, S. and Dryden, W. (1995) *Counselling for Stress Problems*. London: Sage.

Palmer, S. and Lazarus, A.A. (1995) 'In the counsellor's chair: Stephen Palmer interviews Professor Arnold A. Lazarus', *Counselling*, 6 (4): 271–3.

Palmer, S. and Strickland, L. (1995) *Stress Management: a Quick Guide*. Cambridge: Daniels.

Scott, M.J., Stradling, S.G. and Dryden, W. (1995) *Developing Cognitive Behavioural Counselling*. London: Sage.

Spielberger, C.D. (1988) *State-Trait Anger Expression Inventory, Research Edition*. Odessa: Psychological Assessment Resources, Inc.

Spielberger, C.D., Gorsuch, R.L., Lushene, R., Vagg, P.R. and Jacobs, G.A. (1983) *Manual for the State-Trait Anxiety Inventory*. Palo Alto, CA: Consulting Psychologists Press.

Tomm, K. (1984) 'One perspective on the Milan systematic approach. Part II: Description of session format, interviewing style and interventions', *Journal of Marital and Family Therapy*, 10: 253–71.

8 *Reviewing and Evaluating Therapeutic Progress*

Carole Sutton

In a book primarily about assessment, it is appropriate that the greater part of it should focus upon the earliest stages of counselling. This focus, however, should now be balanced by some attention to the later stages of counselling – planning, implementing plans, and finally review and evaluation.

Such a process for practice, whether in counselling, probation work, teaching or community development (or any other human interaction or endeavour), can be helpfully conceptualised using the mnemonic ASPIRE. The process can be thought of as linear:

AS   Assessment
P   Planning
I   Implementation
RE   Review and Evaluation

Alternatively, as is more likely to correspond to what happens, it can be considered cyclical (Figure 8.1).

Earlier chapters have considered assessment, planning and implementing of plans in depth, and we have seen the comprehensiveness and usefulness of the multimodal framework in this respect (see Chapters 6 and 7). In this chapter I shall assume that these stages are well under way, so after some necessary

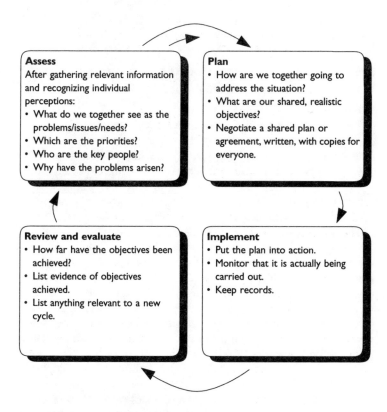

Figure 8.1 *The ASPIRE process as a cycle*

recapitulation of ideas about goal planning, it is now time to consider the stages of review and evaluation.

I shall begin by distinguishing briefly between these two concepts and by clarifying the different processes to which they refer. I shall then remind readers of a number of key concepts which form the context for counselling. After discussing some examples of practice, and how they were reviewed and evaluated, I shall then seek to go beyond a focus upon work with just one individual and show how people seek counselling help for a very wide range of difficulties in living. For these sorts of difficulties I shall suggest some strategies which may be helpful for counsellors who seek to go beyond 'private sorrows' and who wish as well to focus upon 'public issues'. Progress using these techniques can also be reviewed and evaluated.

Reviewing and Evaluating: How Do They Differ?

Reviewing

The process of reviewing is essentially that of monitoring progress, or the lack of it, as client and counsellor work together. It requires the counsellor literally to review (look at again) how the client is faring within the counselling situation. Evidence both from what the client says and from the counsellor's impressions will be available, but a more exact source of information will arise from asking the client frequently, at least at every other meeting, what progress is being made in such a way that it can be measured.

The process of reviewing progress on a regular basis allows clients to say how far they consider they are making progress towards the management or resolution of specified difficulties. Herein lies the advantage of a scale which permits the client to record either progress/improvement or deterioration. Week by week, or according to some other regular interval, changes can be noted – and as appropriate, strategies of helping can be developed, adapted or changed according to discussion with the client. This will be considered further below.

Evaluating

This takes place right at the end of a series of counselling sessions, and is an opportunity for the client to offer a final judgement upon the overall experience. The evidence will be to hand in that at regular intervals the client has informed the counsellor of perceived progress towards agreed goals. It should be a simple matter for both counsellor and client to note the starting points and the end points, and to judge whether there is evidence of improvement or deterioration against each goal. Again, this will be considered further below.

It has been rightly pointed out to me that in view of the power and status of the counsellor, a client could readily be influenced to report improvement even though this was not what was really felt. In these circumstances, and especially if the counsellor is working either within a research framework or as part of a counselling organisation, it should not be too difficult or time consuming a task for each client to be briefly interviewed by an independent person, a researcher or a fellow counsellor, so that the client is able to report material for the evaluation totally confidentially.

Recapitulation of Key Themes

I intend now to highlight some key themes of earlier chapters as a context for considering review and evaluation in more detail. These are:

1   that counselling takes place within a 'systems' framework
2   that it is essential that counsellors use bodies of knowledge or techniques of practice which have been demonstrated as helpful to clients by repeated research
3   that from the uncontrolled proliferation of models of counselling, it does appear that a few key processes underpin effective counselling
4   that using a goal-attainment approach is both ethical and constructive.

First, then, let us note that counselling takes place within a 'systems' framework: that is, human beings exist as part of systems. Looking inwards, they are systems themselves, composed of interacting organs which work together to keep them alive – the respiratory system, the digestive system, the excretory system and so on. Looking outwards, they are part of social systems, such as families, friendship groups, schools, and religious and political organisations. Each individual thus belongs to overlapping networks of relationship and influence and each is affected by happenings within those networks. People are not discrete and separate; they are deeply influenced by circumstances and events which have occurred in the past and which are happening in the present, and they also have profound influence upon other people. Accordingly, changes which occur within our clients are likely to have marked effects upon those with whom they live and work. Counsellors are not therefore accountable solely to their clients; they need also to be aware of the indirect impact of their role upon others.

It follows, as my second important principle, that counsellors should employ only theoretical approaches which have been rigorously evaluated. Literally dozens of approaches to counselling exist but there are few which are grounded upon a body of research of such quality that it is predictable that a given approach will reliably help a person with a specific difficulty. One of the few bodies of convincing research which does exist relates to the 'client-centred' approach: there is indeed some evidence from Rogers (1951), who initiated the approach, from Truax and Carkhuff (1967) and from Atkinson et al. (1993) that this approach has much to offer to people with certain types of difficulty. There is also evidence (see below) of the broad helpfulness of offering people in distress a relationship characterised by warmth, empathy, genuineness and respect.

Similarly, there are few studies which systematically compare the effectiveness of two or more approaches for helping people with similar areas of difficulty, for example, depression or anxiety. In my view it is incumbent upon all counsellors to familiarise themselves with the research evidence for the helpfulness of *any* approach which they employ.

A third important matter is that, among the proliferation of approaches to helping people in distress, it has been established by Atkinson and colleagues (1993) that there are core features common to counselling which appear to carry the greater part of the therapeutic effectiveness. These are:

1   There develops a relationship of warmth and trust in which the counsellor attempts to understand the person and to convey this understanding and respect for the person.

2   The person is offered support by the counsellor. This may be support in coping with a distressing or crisis situation; support in terms of acceptance and respect as an individual; or support in facing past events or traumas.

3   The person experiences a release of tension or a reduction in anxiety which allows him or her to face or talk about a particular problem or problems.

4   The adaptive responses of the person are reinforced. In learning to understand more about themselves and any self-defeating patterns of thought or behaviour, the person is given an opportunity of solving particular problems, improving relationships, etc. The counsellor shares any skills or knowledge which may be appropriate.

The fourth principle which I wish to emphasise is the usefulness of goal setting as a means of enabling clients to clarify at the outset what they are seeking to gain from counselling. This offers both a means of being clear about what client and counsellor are working towards and a means for the client to evaluate how far they have together been successful.

A way of supporting a client in arriving at his or her individual goals using a 'force-field' analysis, which identifies both influences which will facilitate the attainment of the goal and those which will make the attainment difficult, is discussed by Patricia Armstrong in Chapter 6. The role of the counsellor at this stage is to help the client to identify meaningful goals, but ones which are *realistic* and *attainable*. It is essential, for example, for the counsellor to draw attention to over-ambitious goals ('I'll never lose my temper again') and to suggest attainable alternatives ('When I think I'm going to lose my temper, I'll make myself go out and walk up and down for ten minutes'.) It also needs to be borne in mind that several simple, easily attainable goals should be identified so that they can be readily achieved and so that motivation to work towards the more difficult ones can be maintained.

One of the major attractions of this approach is that it is *ethical*. Since the client has indicated what he or she hopes to gain from counselling and has set the agenda, the counsellor has in effect a clear brief. This does not mean that, over time, the client cannot change his or her mind and later the goals which have been targeted; the approach readily accommodates such changes, which may be indicated as the counselling gets under way, and new issues or new concerns become important.

The approach requires a means of enabling the client to measure progress, and thus, as discussed briefly above, a means of reviewing and evaluating progress. This is shown in Figure 8.2. Each goal is set against a simple scale, from −10 through 0 to +10, so that it is absolutely clear what are the targets for counselling. As indicated above, the client stipulates the goals – although of course the counsellor should suggest further areas which his or her experience leads him or her to suggest might be of benefit to the client. It is for the client, however, to specify the nature of each goal – not the counsellor.

Goal Setting within a Systems Framework

Stephen Palmer (1992; see Chapter 7) has already described how, by using the BASIC ID mnemonic, clients can be helped to pinpoint specific aspects of their experience or behaviour which

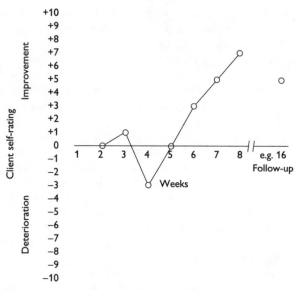

Figure 8.2 *An example of goal setting and evaluation by the client. Goal: that Mrs Jones will feel a renewed sense of confidence in herself*

they wish to change: for example, to change their behaviour by becoming more assertive. He has also shown in the same paper the various strategies which can be employed to assist clients to bring about such changes within a range of modalities. I wish now to develop a related but somewhat more compact model of goal setting which permits a simple method of reviewing and evaluation.

During the initial assessment, which is an activity which I *share* with clients rather than conduct on them, we focus upon the four preliminary questions shown in Figure 8.1. We seek answers to the questions 'What are the concerns?', 'Which are the priorities?', 'Why have they arisen?' and 'Who is involved?' This formulation swiftly helps us focus upon essentials. Clients take the lead in specifying difficulties or wished-for areas of change, but I support them by helping them to be *specific*, by suggesting possible ways of expressing difficulties or by moving from the general to the particular. For example, if someone says 'I want to change the way things are in my life', I can help a client clarify that what she means by this very broad and imprecise aspiration is, for example,

1   I want to feel less isolated.
2   I want to get on better with my daughter.
3   I want to save enough money for a holiday.
4   I want to feel less hopeless and depressed.

It will be apparent that putting things in the tight framework proposed above instantly makes a general situation more manageable – if only because it is now possible for the person concerned to be clear about what precisely would make him or her feel better.

A first step is to help the client to rephrase her statements in a positive format. Thus 'I want to feel less isolated' might become 'I want to make a close friend', or 'I want to get to know the people who live next door so that I can ask them to take an occasional phone message for me', or 'I want to find a new partner in life', or whatever 'feeling less isolated' means specially for this person. Similarly, 'getting on better with my daughter' might mean 'I want her to ask me to look after the baby that I've never seen', or 'I want her to say that the awful row we had can be forgotten', or 'I want her to invite me to meet her new partner.' Saving enough money for a holiday may sound fairly specific, but where, and for how long? For a month's cruise in the Mediterranean or for a long weekend in a self-catering flat somewhere in London? Specifying exactly how much money is to be saved and by when is a far tighter and more manageable proposition. Finally, 'I want to feel less hopeless and depressed' can be helpfully reformulated in a positive and specific form, as 'I want to feel enough self-confidence to find out what I have to do to get my children back from being in care', or 'I want to stop drinking so much', or maybe 'I want to be clearer about whether this is a good relationship for me to be in' – whatever the client says are the *specific sets of circumstances* which will lead her to feel positive rather than depressed.

It is then possible for the client to prioritise the four goals which have emerged. Let us imagine that for this client the first priority in feeling more positive is stopping smoking, since when she smokes she feels guilty and increasingly gloomy. Moreover, this gloominess has undermined the relationship with her daughter, and contributed to the lack of contact between them. The next priority is to save £200 towards a holiday in Spain in a year's time. The third is to improve relationships with her daughter. The fourth goal has become twofold: to make contact with neighbours with a view to asking them to receive an occasional phone call, and also to make a friend to go out with occasionally. The goals are then re-written in a new order of priority. At the time of writing each one scores 0.

During the subsequent weeks, counsellor and client work together towards the attainment of the goals. As the client's primary goal is to feel less depressed, it is the counsellor's responsibility to formulate a hypothesis for the depression: that is, to discuss possible answers to the question 'Why has this depression arisen?' The first source of information is of course the client herself: why does she think she is depressed? If her exploring of this area indicates that her depression is of fairly recent onset, accompanying the loss of a job, an income and all the associated satisfactions of employment, then the counsellor's suggestions for helping are likely to be practical and to be based upon research for helping people experiencing short-term depression (see Jenkins et al., 1992). If, however, the client talks of long-standing depression stemming from difficult rela-tionships in childhood or from emotional or sexual abuse, then a counsellor trained in cognitive approaches would be likely to explore her beliefs and attitudes about the event(s), her beliefs about herself and issues related to self-esteem. Even in such circumstances, it is possible to agree goals which will constitute a focus for client and counsellor to work towards together – such as 'I want to talk to my mother about why she put me in care for two years' or 'I want to meet the man who abused me and tell him what it has done to me.'

Reviewing Progress against Goals

It has become my practice – after an initial meeting, or occa-sionally two, focusing upon assessment, and assuming clients indicate that they wish to proceed – to offer a sequence of five further weekly meetings during which time planning and the implementing of those plans can take place. If we proceed, as we usually do, then a simple written agreement is often completed at this stage so that times and numbers of future meetings are clear. We may well also include the goals of the counselling as the client perceives them at that stage. We first put the perceived areas of difficulty into an order of priority and then turn them, as described above, into specific tasks to be undertaken or problems to be solved.

Having this 'agenda' in front of us typically is seen as very helpful by clients, who have often spent time and energy berating themselves or other people for their difficulties and who have lacked a conceptual framework for moving forward. A goal-setting approach of looking at their difficulties, and recognising that the agenda has come from them, not from me, typically reduces anxiety, as Atkinson and colleagues (1993) suggest. A key point is that I have not 'diagnosed' their difficulties; we have worked on clarifying them together. This new perspective also generates motivation and an optimism that at least some of the difficulties can be overcome.

Clients themselves seem to know many of the answers to the main question which arises in the planning stage: 'How are these goals to be achieved?' My contributions here have often taken one or more of the following forms:

- *To act as a 'sounding board'*   Clients may wish to explore with me different courses of action, and the various possible outcomes of each upon other parts of the systems to which they belong, for example, their families or their work colleagues.
- *To make suggestions from my knowledge of the research*   Examples are the consistent finding that the practice of regular relaxation is beneficial for people who experience much general anxiety (Jacobson, 1938) or the firm evidence that depression can be much relieved by regular physical exercise (Thayer et al., 1994).
- *To give support in times of difficulty and setback*   Here my experience is that often people make considerable progress towards their goals early in the sequence, but then 'lose their way' either through being too ambitious or through meeting the inevitable difficulties which arise when people try to manage their lives differently. I can give them anticipatory guidance that such difficulties are likely to arise, and then when they do can recommend lowering their sights a little.
- *To build in occasions when success is inevitable*   This refers to situations where clients have set themselves targets for success which are too high and are downcast by the failure which has inevitably followed. Here it is helpful to make use

of a 'graded hierarchy', a ladder of success in which the lowest steps are so easy to attain that the person is bound to succeed. For example, a person trying to save money, who has already accumulated a small sum, might agree that for one week his goal will simply be not to take any money out of his account – in the knowledge that he couldn't anyway because a month's notice is required! Sometimes this *engineering of success* can become an opportunity for creative light-heartedness, and there is laughter and fun as we develop some 'impossible to fail' goals. The exercise, however, has a serious point in that the person concerned cannot fail to experience the positive feedback of success – which in turn motivates him or her to attempt the next (modest) challenge.

The Goal-Attainment Approach: the Process of Review

The process of reviewing is very straightforward when goals have been previously negotiated between client(s) and counsellor: progress against goals can be literally plotted on simple graphs week by week, with the *client* stating the progress towards each goal that he or she considers has been made. The entries may or may not be in accord with the counsellor's perception; in my own case entries have been in accord. (See Figure 8.2, which represents a typical goal.)

Every so often, say every three or four weeks, if counselling is continuing that long, it is appropriate to take a look at whether some goals have been already attained, whether some are likely to be attained or whether some have been worded too ambitiously or are now seen as inappropriate. It is perfectly in order to adapt such goals to meet the changed circumstances; we usually both initial and date any changes as an indication that the adjustment was by common consent.

I am aware, of course, that in some counselling situations there will be occasions when the person experiences great distress, and may say that this distress cannot be said to constitute progress. This may be so, but an experienced counsellor should be able to anticipate occasions when there is likely to be distress, for example when discussing trauma or bereavement. If distress can be anticipated then the client need not necessarily feel that experiencing pain, of itself, is not indicative of progress. It is to be hoped that the counsellor will be sufficiently skilled to be able to support the person through such a time of distress so that recovery or adjustment can be resumed thereafter. If not, then this is likely to be shown on the graph: steps should be taken to discuss developments with one's supervisor as a matter of urgency.

The Goal-Attainment Approach: the Process of Evaluation

As already indicated, using a goal-setting approach means that the effectiveness of the counselling offered is apparent week by week. As the end of the sequence draws near, it is a straight-forward matter to consider each goal and for the client to state how far he or she has come towards attaining the final target. This is the process of evaluation.

One can use the following scale as an index:

    7+   achieved to a very high standard
    6+   achieved to a high standard
    5+   achieved to a moderate standard
    4+   achieved to a satisfactory standard
    <4   not achieved

It may be possible to state, on the basis of evidence before one's eyes, that, for example,

Of five goals: two have been met to a very high standard
            one has been met to a high standard, and
            one has been achieved to a moderate standard, but
            one has not been achieved.

I have never yet worked with anyone who used this goal-setting approach and who stated at the evaluation that any situation in respect of which we had developed a goal was worse than at the outset. To be sure, during the course of counselling, some situations have become temporarily worse than at the beginning. On one particular occasion, one young person had a terrible week, when progress towards each and every goal took a downward plunge, but with support, she was able to avoid being thrown off course by the events of that week, and at our following meeting progress towards goals resumed an upward movement.

Had this renewed improvement not taken place, however, we could have done one of several things. For example, we could have:

1   paid particular attention to the young woman's self-esteem. It has been my experience that it is almost always appropriate to include as one goal the raising of the self-esteem of the person concerned. People who come to see counsellors are almost always discouraged, bruised by the world and by people in it (sometimes literally). No one with whom I have worked has rejected my suggestion that one goal might be 'That I shall feel I am a person of greater worth and value than I do at present.' Enhancement of self-esteem seems to be one of the effects of the way the counsellor behaves towards the client (with respect, warmth and empathy) but it is also a direct result of things that the client does. So active attempts to raise the self-esteem of clients usually has directly beneficial effects.
2   discussed whether some specific part of her difficulties was preventing progress in other areas; for example, whether depression or perhaps anxiety was undermining her ability to take the other initiatives she had intended. In this case, 'structuring success' might be helpful, or perhaps specific steps might be necessary to address these difficulties, such as cognitive therapy to deal with repetitious and negative self-statements.
3   considered whether the initial assessment was wrong, and whether I had neglected some crucial aspect of what the young woman was telling me, leading to a shared but none the less faulty formulation of her difficulties. If this appeared to be the case, both from the evidence in front of us and in the light of what she was now telling me, it would have been necessary to undertake a completely fresh assessment, followed by a fresh planning stage and so on.

A further advantage of this way of working, employing a scale against which progress towards each goal can be evaluated, is that it lends itself to undertaking research. For example, if one wished to compare two strategies of intervention for depression, one could, assuming that all the ethical requirements had been met, compare the 'before' and 'after' scores of substantial numbers of people following the two strategies and see which one proved more beneficial, as measured by the scores reported at the end of the intervention by participants. These data thus lend themselves to statistical analysis.

This way of working also calls for a follow-up meeting between client and counsellor (see Figure 8.1) so that they can ascertain whether the client judges that any improvement achieved has been maintained. To be sure, in some circumstances the counsellor will need to check whether any practical strategy which had been agreed, such as that the client will undertake physical exercise, is still being practised. Often several 'booster' sessions may be found to be useful.

The Goal-Attainment Approach: Working with More Than One Person

As I have made the case elsewhere (Sutton, 1987) people do not seek help from counsellors for difficulties pertaining exclusively to themselves. In that individuals are part of systems (families, work groups, friendship groups and so on) they bring to counsellors problems concerning the care of people with long-term illness, mental health disorders or dementia; they bring problems of relationships with spouses or partners, with adolescents or with stepchildren; they bring worries about financial problems, and concerns about their own or a family member's drinking patterns. Almost never are a client's difficulties neatly circumscribed and amenable to a single body of 'theory' or 'therapy'. We need an extensive repertoire of knowledge and skills for a huge array of people with an even wider array of difficulties.

To begin with, it is essential that we familiarise ourselves with the wide range of services and resources which are increasingly available in the community. We need to know of agencies which support care-givers, over and above the hard-pressed social services departments, and where help with alcohol difficulties is available; we need to know what the voluntary organisations like MIND and the Family Service Units can offer and where Citizens' Advice Bureaux are located; and we need to know where debt counselling help is available – and a dozen other sources of help and support.

In addition, we should not be blinkered by our training in work primarily with individuals so that we neglect the fact that the context of many 'private troubles' is a 'public issue'. So, rather than focus exclusively upon an individual's response to stress, it may be very appropriate to consider with that person whether their employers are in fact asking too much of them. Or, rather than focus exclusively upon the emotions generated by a person made redundant, one might help them appreciate that the redundancy is in no sense their 'fault', but is rather the impact of central government policy concerning, say, the future of the coal industry.

A Repertoire of Skills for Multifocal Counselling

I use the term 'multifocal counselling' in part to complement the term 'multimodal counselling' (see Chapter 7) but also to emphasise features of counselling which go beyond the focus upon just one individual and accommodate the broader range of concerns which I have just described. The counsellor may need a range of knowledge and skills for such situations which go beyond those often taught on counselling courses, but the goal-setting model is equally relevant here, and practice in these areas can also be both reviewed and evaluated.

Some specific areas of skill and knowledge for 'multifocal counselling' might include:

1 Ability to engage two or more people in working together. These may be spouses, partners or members of family groups, such as parents and young people.
2 Ability to undertake assessment, planning, implementing of plans, review and evaluation, for example with partners in relationships, and with family groups including stepfamilies.
3 Ability to negotiate working agreements with these groups (see Sutton, 1994).
4 Ability to work with groups of people from minority backgrounds. This requires an extensive knowledge base, as well as sensitivity and powers of empathy.
5 Ability to work with people coping with disability and with the implications of disability.
6 Ability to understand issues of identity in respect of gay and lesbian people and those from minority groups.
7 Awareness of issues of discrimination, as experienced by many women and other groups who typically lack power.

Reviewing and Evaluating Work in These Contexts

The model proposed above holds good with these more demanding situations. The skills required of the counsellor in these contexts are indeed greater than for work with an individual because of the necessity of keeping people who may be at odds with each other engaged in the counselling exercise; however, the practice of enabling clients to state what they (all) want to gain from the experience of counselling is a valid one. In such a situation a brief written agreement can be very helpful to all concerned. Some goals may be common to all participants and others can be particularised for each individual. In the latter case, one family member might offer to assist others in helping them achieve their goals. I offer below an example of a goal which might be common to all members of a family and then an example of goals which individuals might choose.

A Goal Common to All Family Members:
Overall aim
To reduce the number of family rows by 50 per cent.

Specific Goals
1   During a baseline period of two weeks, to record the number of arguments lasting one minute or more between two or more family members.
2   During this baseline period, to record:
   (a)   who are the participants in the arguments
   (b)   what the arguments are about
   (c)   the cues or triggers for the arguments
   (d)   how long the arguments last.
3   After the baseline period, to discuss how to use a problem-solving approach (Spivack et al., 1976) for reducing the number of arguments.
4   Over the next fortnight, to try out the strategies arising from the problem-solving approach and to continue to record the number of rows so that these can be compared with the baseline figure.

Typically, a great deal of information arises from this way of tackling difficulties which a skilled counsellor can put to good use when trying to help families. Above all, there is evidence and data to which to turn when it is time to review progress. If no progress at all has been made, then an alternative to the problem-solving approach can be employed and that too can be reviewed and evaluated.

Goals with which Individuals within a Family or Group Might Identify

A parent

1 To spend 20 minutes talking without interruption with spouse or partner.
2 To go for a walk with spouse/partner for at least an hour weekly.
3 To eat a meal which he/she has not prepared once weekly.
4 To be supported by partner at least in public over decisions she/he has made concerning the children.

A teenager

1 To bring a friend home for a meal once weekly.
2 Not to have their friends criticised for a full week.
3 After once giving truthful information about where they are going, not to be cross-questioned further when they return.
4 To be encouraged, not nagged, to do homework.

In all these cases, *the people concerned are the ones who review and evaluate progress*; the counsellor acts to facilitate each person's attainment of their goals.

Practice Points: Contextual

Remember how much influence and power you have as a counsellor.

Remember that some people have not the faintest idea what the word 'counselling' means and have no idea of what they are supposed to do when they meet you. A simple description of what often happens in counselling can be invaluable.

Remember that counselling takes place within a legislative framework.

Counselling as a formal procedure is a Western phenomenon. Undertake training to equip yourself to work with people from a range of other communities.

Keep yourself up to date with the research literature.

Practice Points: Procedural

Try to share your assessment of the person's difficulty with the person concerned as you go along. 'It seems to me that . . . . Does that make sense to you or not?'

Show the notes you have made to the person concerned so that he or she is as fully participant in the counselling process as possible.

Have a clock located where you can both see it clearly. If necessary, have two clocks.

Let counselling be an educational as well as a developmental process: for example, explain the nature of the anxiety response, if this would itself ease anxiety.

Ask for feedback from the client at least every two sessions upon whether the counselling is proving helpful or not, and what aspects are particularly helpful.

Try to summarise the main points covered at the end of a counselling session.

Conclusion: Adapting the Goal-Attainment Approach to Any Theory of Counselling

As I wrote in my earlier paper (Sutton, 1987):

I hope it will be apparent from the above that using a model in which goals are negotiated at the outset in no way precludes the use of any particular theory of counselling or therapy. During the stage of intervention any theory at all which the counsellor feels is ethically appropriate to the needs of the client may be employed. But it is employed in such a way that its helpfulness can be evaluated.

In the intervention period then one might see counsellors employing not only ideas from client-centred therapy, principles of transactional analysis, rational-emotive therapy, Gestalt and behaviour therapy – but engaged also in the practicalities of giving information and putting people in touch with services. The goal-attainment approach is not yet another theory of counselling; it is a way of structuring intervention, and then of evaluating it.

Since I wrote the above passage, my paper about the goal-attainment approach has been reprinted on a number of occasions and the strategy is being increasingly used as a simple but effective way of reviewing and evaluating practice. My hopes that it would be seen to be ethical, and found to be both practical and empowering of clients, seem to be coming true.

References

Atkinson, R.L., Atkinson, R.C., Smith, E.E. and Bem, D. (1993) *Introduction to Psychology*. Harcourt Brace Jovanovich.

Jacobson, E.J. (1938) *Progressive Relaxation*. Chicago: University of Chicago Press.

Jenkins, R., Newton, J. and Young, R. (1992) *The Prevention of Depression and Anxiety*. London: HMSO.

Palmer, S. (1992) 'Multimodal assessment and therapy. A systematic, technically eclectic approach to counselling, psychotherapy and stress management', *Counselling*, 3 (4): 220–4.

Rogers, C. (1951) *Client-Centred Therapy*. Boston: Houghton Mifflin.

Spivack, G., Platt, J.J. and Shure, M. (1976) *The Problem-Solving Approach to Adjustment*. San Francisco: Jossey-Bass.

Sutton, C. (1987) 'The evaluation of counselling: a goal-attainment approach', *Counselling*, May: 14–20.

Sutton, C. (1994) *Social Work, Community Work and Psychology*. Leicester: British Psychological Society.

Thayer, R.E., Newman, J.R. and McClain, T.M. (1994) 'Self-regulation of mood: strategies for changing a bad mood, raising energy and reducing tension', *Journal of Personality and Social Psychology*, 67: 910–25.

Truax, C. and Carkhuff, R. (1967) *Towards Effective Counseling and Psychotherapy*. Chicago: Aldine.

Postscript

Hopefully this book has given the reader some insight into a range of issues on client assessment. Inevitably some issues were not included although it was not the intention to write a complete handbook of client assessment. However, with this idea in mind, we would be interested to hear from readers about what subjects they would like us to cover in such a handbook. Please write to us at the following address with your feedback and ideas:

Stephen Palmer and Gladeana McMahon
Centre for Stress Management
156 Westcombe Hill
London
SE3 7DH

Appendix
Multimodal Life History Inventory

The purpose of this inventory is to obtain a comprehensive picture of your background. In psychotherapy records are necessary since they permit a more thorough dealing with one's problems. By completing these questions as fully and as accurately as you can, you will facilitate your therapeutic program. You are requested to answer these routine questions in your own time instead of using up your actual consulting time (please feel free to use extra sheets if you need additional answer space).

It is understandable that you might be concerned about what happens to the information about you because much or all of this information is highly personal. *Case records are strictly confidential.*

General Information

Date. Name. Address. Telephone numbers.
Age. Occupation. Sex. Date of birth. Place of birth. Religion.
Height. Weight. Does your weight fluctuate? If yes, by how much?
Do you have a family physician? Name of family physician.
   Telephone number. By whom were you referred?

Copyright © 1991 by Arnold A. Lazarus and Clifford N. Lazarus. Reprinted by permission of the Research Press, 2612 North Mattis Avenue, Champaign, Illinois 61821.

Marital status: single, engaged, married, separated, divorced, widowed, living with someone, remarried (how many times?)

Do you live in: house, room, apartment, other?

With whom do you live: self, parents, spouse, roommate, child(ren), friend(s), others (specify)?

What sort of work are you doing now? Does your present work satisfy you? If no, please explain. What kind of jobs have you held in the past?

Have you been in therapy before or received any professional assistance for your problems?

Have you ever been hospitalized for psychological/psychiatric problems? If yes, when and where?

Have you ever attempted suicide? Does any member of your family suffer from an 'emotional' or 'mental disorder'? Has any relative attempted or committed suicide?

Personal and Social History

Father: name, age, occupation, health. If deceased, give his age at time of death. How old were you at the time? Cause of death.

Mother: name, age, occupation, health. If deceased, give her age at time of death. How old were you at the time? Cause of death.

Siblings: Age(s) of brother(s), age(s) of sister(s). Any significant details about siblings.

If you were not brought up by your parents, who raised you and between what years?

Give a description of your father's (or father substitute's) personality and his attitude toward you (past and present).

Give a description of your mother's (or mother substitute's) personality and her attitude toward you (past and present).

In what ways were you disciplined or punished by your parents? Give an impression of your home atmosphere (i.e., the home in which you grew up). Mention state of compatibility between parents and between children. Were you able to confide in your parents? Basically, did you feel loved and respected by your parents?

If you have a stepparent, give your age when your parent remarried. Has anyone (parents, relatives, friends) ever interfered in your marriage, occupation, etc.? If yes, please describe briefly.

Scholastic strengths. Scholastic weaknesses. What was the last grade completed (or highest degree)?

Check any of the following that applied during your childhood/ adolescence: happy childhood, unhappy childhood, emotional/ behavior problems, legal trouble, death in family, medical problems, ignored, not enough friends, school problems, financial problems, strong religious convictions, drug use, used alcohol, severely punished, sexually abused, severely bullied or teased, eating disorder, others.

Description of Presenting Problems

State in your own words the nature of your main problems.

On the [following] scale, please estimate the severity of your problem(s): mildly upsetting, moderately upsetting, very severe, extremely severe, totally incapacitating.

When did your problems begin? What seems to worsen your problems? What have you tried that has been helpful?

How satisfied are you with your life as a whole these days? (not at all satisfied) 1, 2, 3, 4, 5, 6, 7 (very satisfied)

How would you rate your overall level of tension during the past month? (relaxed) 1, 2, 3, 4, 5, 6, 7 (tense)

Expectations Regarding Therapy

In a few words, what do you think therapy is all about?

How long do you think your therapy should last?

What personal qualities do you think the ideal therapist should possess?

Modality Analysis of Current Problems

The following section is designed to help you describe your current problems in greater detail and to identify problems that might otherwise go unnoticed. This will enable us to design a comprehensive treatment program and tailor it to your specific needs. The following section is organized according to the seven modalities of behaviors, feelings, physical sensations, images, thoughts, interpersonal relationships, and biological factors.

Behaviors

Check any of the following behaviors that often apply to you: overeat, take drugs, unassertive, odd behavior, drink too much, work too hard, procrastination, impulsive reactions, loss of control, suicidal attempts, compulsions, smoke, withdrawal, nervous tics, concentration difficulties, sleep disturbance, phobic avoidance, spend too much money, can't keep a job, insomnia, take too many risks, lazy, eating problems, aggressive behavior, crying, outbursts of temper, others.

What are some special talents or skills that you feel proud of?
What would you like to start doing? What would you like to stop doing?
How is your free time spent?
What kind of hobbies or leisure activities do you enjoy or find relaxing?
Do you have trouble relaxing or enjoying weekends and vacations? If yes, please explain.
If you could have any two wishes, what would they be?

Feelings

Check any of the following feelings that often apply to you: angry, annoyed, sad, depressed, anxious, fearful, panicky, energetic, envious, guilty, happy, conflicted, shameful, regretful, hopeless, hopeful, helpless, relaxed, jealous, unhappy, bored, restless, lonely, contented, excited, optimistic, tense, others.

List your five main fears.
What are some positive feelings you have experienced recently?
When are you most likely to lose control of your feelings?
Describe any situations that make you feel calm or relaxed:

Physical Sensations

Check any of the following physical sensations that often apply to you: abdominal pain, pain or burning with urination, menstrual difficulties, headaches, dizziness, palpitations, muscle spasms, tension, sexual disturbances, unable to relax, bowel disturbances, tingling, numbness, stomach trouble, tics, fatigue, twitches, back pain, tremors, fainting spells, hear things, watery eyes, flushes, nausea, skin problems, dry mouth, burning or itching skin, chest pains, rapid heart beat, don't like to be touched, blackouts, excessive sweating, visual disturbances, hearing problems, others.

What sensations are: pleasant for you? unpleasant for you?

Images

Check any of the following that apply to you.

I picture myself: being happy, being hurt, not coping, succeeding, losing control, being followed, being talked about, being aggressive, being helpless, hurting others, being in charge, failing, being trapped, being laughed at, being promiscuous, others.

I have: pleasant sexual images, unpleasant childhood images, negative body image, unpleasant sexual images, lonely images, seduction images, images of being loved, others.

Describe a very pleasant image, mental picture, or fantasy.

Describe a very unpleasant image, mental picture, or fantasy.

Describe your image of a completely 'safe place'.

Describe any persistent or disturbing images that interfere with your daily functioning.

How often do you have nightmares?

Thoughts

Check each of the following that you might use to describe yourself: intelligent, confident, worthwhile, ambitious, sensitive, loyal, trustworthy, full of regrets, worthless, a nobody, useless, evil, crazy, morally degenerate, considerate, deviant, unattractive, unlovable, inadequate, confused, ugly, stupid, naive, honest, incompetent, horrible thoughts, conflicted, concentration difficulties, memory problems, attractive, can't make decisions, suicidal ideas, persevering, good sense of humor, hard working, undesirable, lazy, untrustworthy, dishonest, others.

What do you consider to be your craziest thought or idea?

Are you bothered by thoughts that occur over and over again? If yes, what are these thoughts?

What worries do you have that may negatively affect your mood or behavior?

On each of the following items, please circle the number that most accurately reflects your opinions [scale against each item: 1, strongly disagree; 2, disagree; 3, neutral; 4, agree; 5, strongly agree]:

I should not make mistakes.

I should be good at everything I do.

When I do not know something, I should pretend that I do.

I should not disclose personal information.
I am a victim of circumstances.
My life is controlled by outside forces.
Other people are happier than I am.
It is very important to please other people.
Play it safe; don't take any risks.
I don't deserve to be happy.
If I ignore my problems, they will disappear.
It is my responsibility to make other people happy.
I should strive for perfection.
Basically, there are two ways of doing things – the right way and the wrong way.
I should never be upset.

Interpersonal Relationships
Friendships

Do you make friends easily? Do you keep them?
Did you date much during high school? College?
Were you ever bullied or severely teased?
Describe any relationship that gives you: joy; grief.
Rate the degree to which you generally feel relaxed and comfortable in social situations: (very relaxed) 1, 2, 3, 4, 5, 6, 7, (very anxious).
Do you have one or more friends with whom you feel comfortable sharing your most private thoughts?

Marriage (or a Committed Relationship)

How long did you know your spouse before your engagement? How long were you engaged before you got married? How long have you been married?
What is your spouse's age? His/her occupation?
Describe your spouse's personality. What do you like most about your spouse? What do you like least about your spouse?
What factors detract from your marital satisfaction?
On the [following] scale, please indicate how satisfied you are with your marriage: (very dissatisfied) 1, 2, 3, 4, 5, 6, 7, (very satisfied).
How do you get along with your partner's friends and family? (very poorly) 1, 2, 3, 4, 5, 6, 7, (very well).
How many children do you have? Please give their names and ages.

Do any of your children present special problems? If yes, please describe.

Any significant details about a previous marriage(s)?

Sexual Relationships

Describe your parents' attitude toward sex. Was sex discussed in your home?

When and how did you derive your first knowledge of sex?

When did you first become aware of your own sexual impulses?

Have you ever experienced any anxiety or guilt arising out of sex or masturbation? If yes, please explain.

Any relevant details regarding your first or subsequent sexual experiences?

Is your present sex life satisfactory? If no, please explain.

Provide information about any significant homosexual reactions or relationships.

Please note any sexual concerns not discussed above.

Other Relationships

Are there any problems in your relationships with people at work? If yes, please describe.

Please complete the following: one of the ways people hurt me is . . .; I could shock you by . . .; my spouse (or boyfriend/girlfriend) would described me as . . .; my best friend thinks I am . . .; people who dislike me . . . .

Are you currently troubled by any past rejections or loss of a love relationship? If yes, please explain.

Biological Factors

Do you have any current concerns about your physical health? If yes, please specify.

Please list any medications you are currently taking.

Do you eat three well-balanced meals each day?

Do you get regular physical exercise? If yes, what type and how often?

Please list any significant medical problems that apply to you or to members of your family.

Please describe any surgery you have had (give dates).

Please describe any physical handicap(s) you have.

Menstrual History

Age at first period. Where you informed? Did it come as a shock?

Are you regular? Duration. Do you have pain? Do your periods affect your moods? Date of last period.

Check any of the following that apply to you [scale against each item: never; rarely; occasionally; frequently; daily]:
muscle weakness, tranquilizers, diuretics, diet pills, marijuana, hormones, sleeping pills, aspirin, cocaine, pain killers, narcotics, stimulants, hallucinogens (e.g., LSD), laxatives, cigarettes, tobacco (specify), coffee, alcohol, birth control pills, vitamins, undereat, overeat, eat junk foods, diarrhea, constipation, gas, indigestion, nausea, vomiting, heartburn, dizziness, palpitations, fatigue, allergies, high blood pressure, chest pain, shortness of breath, insomnia, sleep too much, fitful sleep, early morning awakening, earaches, headaches, backaches, bruise or bleed easily, weight problems, others.

Structural Profile

Directions: rate yourself on the following dimensions on a seven-point scale with 1 being the lowest and 7 being the highest.

Behaviors Some people may be described as 'doers' – they are action oriented, they like to busy themselves, get things done, take on various projects. How much of a doer are you?

Feelings Some people are very emotional and may or may not express it. How emotional are you? How deeply do you feel things? How passionate are you?

Physical sensations Some people attach a lot of value to sensory experiences, such as sex, food, music, art, and other 'sensory delights'. Others are very much aware of minor aches, pains, and discomforts. How 'tuned into' your sensations are you?

Mental images How much fantasy or daydreaming do you engage in? This is separate from thinking or planning. This is 'thinking in pictures', visualizing real or imagined experiences, letting your mind roam. How much are you into imagery?

Thoughts Some people are very analytical and like to plan things. They like to reason things through. How much of a 'thinker' and 'planner' are you?

Interpersonal relationships How important are other people to you? This is your self-rating as a social being. How important are close friendships to you, the tendency to gravitate toward people, the desire for intimacy? The opposite of this is being a 'loner'.

Biological factors   Are you healthy and health conscious? Do you avoid bad habits like smoking, too much alcohol, drinking a lot of coffee, overeating, etc.? Do you exercise regularly, get enough sleep, avoid junk food, and generally take care of your body?

Please describe any significant childhood (or other) memories and experiences you think your therapist should be aware of.

Editors and Contributors

The Editors

Stephen Palmer is Director of the Centre for Stress Management and the Centre for Multimodal Therapy, London. He is a Chartered Counselling Psychologist, a UKCP registered psychotherapist, a BAC Fellow, an Associate Fellow of the Institute of Rational-Emotive Therapy, New York, and a certified supervisor for training in REBT. He edits *Counselling Psychology Review* and *The Rational Emotive Behaviour Therapist* and has authored or edited 13 books and manuals. He edits three book series including *Stress Counselling* (Cassell). His recent books include *Counselling: The BAC Counselling Reader* (with Dainow and Milner 1996), *Dealing with People Problems* (with Burton 1996) and *Stress Management and Counselling* (1996 with Dryden).

Gladeana McMahon is a BAC accredited counsellor and recognised counselling supervisor, is a BABCP accredited cognitive-behavioural psychotherapist and is UKCP registered. She has run a successful private practice since 1988 providing counselling, training and counselling supervision and has worked in a variety of voluntary, medical, statutory and private sector settings. She is the author of *Starting Your Own Private Practice* (1994).

The Contributors

Patricia Armstrong has a BSc (Hons) in Psychology and an MSc in Counselling Psychology. She currently works as a Manager/ Counsellor for an alcohol counselling agency in Kent. She supervises students on Counselling Diploma and MSc Counselling Psychology courses. She also guest lectures at universities in London and Kent. Patricia runs a private practice from home.

Mark Aveline has been a consultant medical psychotherapist in Nottingham since 1974. His chief interests are in the development of a range of effective psychotherapies, suitable for NHS practice, and teaching the necessary skills at undergraduate, post-qualification and specialist levels. He is a member of the Governing Board of the United Kingdom Council for Psychotherapy (1992–), Chair of the Training Committee of South Trent Training in Dynamic Psychotherapy (1984–), President of the British Association for Counselling (1994–), Chair of the Psychotherapy Training Specialist Advisory Committee of the Royal College of Psychiatrists (1995–) and UK Vice-President of the Society for Psychotherapy Research (1996–). His books include *Group Therapy in Britain* (1988), *From Medicine to psychotherapy* (1992) and *Research Foundations for Psychotherapy Practice* (1995).

Berni Curwen is a cognitive-behavioural psychotherapist accredited by the BABCP and registered with the United Kingdom Council for Psychotherapy. She has a psychiatric nurse background and has worked in both the NHS and private practice.

Peter Ruddell is a cognitive-behavioural psychotherapist accredited by the BABCP and the Association for Rational Emotive Behaviour Therapists and registered with the United Kingdom Council for Psychotherapy. He has worked in both the private and voluntary sectors.

Carole Sutton is a Principal Lecturer in Psychology at De Montfort University, Leicester, where she teaches psychology and counselling skills. She is also a Chartered Counselling Psychologist. She is particularly interested in the evaluation of practice and is a former Chair of the Research Sub-committee of the British Association for Counselling. Her publications include *A Handbook of Research for the Helping Professions* and *Social Work, Community Work and Psychology*.

Index